I've Been 16 for 34 Years™

a BoomerTweener™ memoir

Julie Johnson Oliver

First Edition

Groveland Branch Press
I've Been 16 for 34 Years™
a BoomerTweener™ memoir

by Julie Johnson Oliver

Published by:
Groveland Branch Press
P.O. Box 460
Fall City, Washington 98024 U.S.A.
http://grovelandbranchpress.com

All rights reserved. No part of this book may be reproduced or transmitted in any form or by any means, electronic or mechanical, including photocopying, recording or by any information storage and retrieval system, without written permission from the author or publisher.

Sorry Wrong Number - Copyright © 1948 by Lucille Fletcher. Reprinted by permission of William Morris, LLC on behalf of the Author.

Cover photo – John Carleton/iStock.com

ISBN, print ed. 978-0-578-00086-2
ISBN, PDF ED.
ISBN, LIT ed.
First Printing 2008
Printed in the United States of America

Library of Congress Cataloging-in-Publication Data
Library of Congress Control Number: 2009907538
Oliver, Julie Johnson
I've Been 16 for 34 Years a BoomerTweener memoir/Julie Johnson Oliver—1st edition.
P.cm.
Includes bibliographical references (p.)
ISBN 978-0-578-00086-2
  1. Humor—United States
  2. Memoir—baby boomer
  3. Inspiration

Table of Contents

Acknowledgements - 6
Dedication - 7
Disclaimer Warning - 8
Introduction - 9
The Sleep of Hell - 13
Stiff Competition - 15
Email Audition - 21
George Gray - 28
Country Road Take Me Home - 29
PMS – The Not-So-Pretty-Picture Book - 35
The Terrible Horrible Tinkley Gangrenous Day - 45
Big Humiliation - 55
Queen on a Hot Tin Roof - 59
One Cute Boy and One Fast Dance - 71
Retro - 77
The List of Places I've Waited - 79
Bad Hair Day - 87
I'm Just A Little Black Rain Cloud - 93
Yummy, Yummy, Yummy - 99
Jeri and Julie's Funtime Caftan Pattern - 103
Running Away To The North Bend Motel - 113
Chicken Fat - 123
30 Rules for Living in Idaho - 131
Nearsighted - 139
Terrible Phone Prank - 147
Fleeting - 152
Battle of the Bands - 153
Whoa Back and Cowboy Up - 161
Wove, Twue Wove - 165
One Blind Mouse - 178
Everything I Know I Learned in a Crab Pot - 179
Oh, The Weather Outside Is Frightful - 185
Water Fitness - 191
Home Ick - 201
Just A Little Poke - 209 The Daring Young Girl on The Flying Trapeze - 217
BoomerTweener - 223
Throwing Up – 229

Acknowledgements

Thanks to my good friends Sue, Lindsay, Heidi, Lucy, and Amelia for reading rough drafts and giving me feedback. Thank you to Elisabeth Swan for proofreading. Thank you to Jennifer Lynn Johnson for meticulous editing.

Thanks for inspiration from Jeri, my best girlfriend of 34+ years, and for our pact made three decades ago to maintain *foxy bodies, clean houses, and sweet spirits.*

Thanks to Molly Christensen Oliver for book cover and logo designs.

Thanks to Brandon Gunter for saving the life of my hard drive, which held years of accumulated computer files. (That I am now properly backing up on a regular basis.)

Thanks to all my good doctors, Dr. Kais Faddah and Dr. Ladd Carlston, who saved the life of my spine, allowing me to keep my head up and type; and Dr. Ann McCombs, Claudia Pétursson, and Paula G. Dolinko, my current lifesavers.

Thanks to successful strangers I've never met or spoken to, like Dan Poynter, Donny Deutsch, and Kim Lavine, who motivated me to actually complete this project. Someday I'd like to buy you each a Dreamsicle. And you could maybe buy me a pony or a Porsche. Your choice.

Photography Credits

The photos on pages 41, 76, 78, 137, 177, 190, 227 are by Mark Thomas Oliver. I thank him for his generosity in allowing his fine art to be used in this book.

The photos on pages 14, 20, 27, 33, 43, 58, 86, 98, 111, 112, 122, 129, 138, 146, 160, 164, 184, 200 top, 208, 215, 233 are from Julie J. Oliver.

The rest are by other photographers who have sworn me to secrecy.

Some of these photos can be enlarged into fine art prints or posters. If you are interested in ordering prints, please see the information at the back of the book.

Dedication

To my true love and best friend of 32+ years: my husband, the finest funny man I know.

To my wonderful children, living quiet lives of goodness, service, strength, and commitment. They have helped raise me. And to their spouses, our fantastic "new" kids.

To my gorgeous grandchildren who make me giggle and give me lubba lubba.

To my priceless family heritage, which includes brothers, parents, and grandparents, among other assorted nuts in my family tree.

All of these people are treasures. Joy and contentment wash over me as I rub elbows with them.

And to all of my readers...
may we each conquer the fear of looking stupid
and find the courage to live in truth.

Disclaimer Warning

This book is designed to entertain through humor and a little personal history that contains universal themes you might relate to. It is sold with the knowledge that the publisher and author are not engaged in rendering health, nutritional, fitness, legal, or relationship services. If expert help is required in your life, you should call competent professionals...or maybe Ghostbusters.

It is not the purpose of these essays to keep you happy, help you lose weight, get you married (or divorced), produce your grandchildren, housebreak your pets, or win a "Dancing With The...Commoner" competition.

Every effort has been made to tipe gud, purmit gud, and 4mat gud and akeratlee. If you find any mistakes here, they must be there for you; as is a little literary license for humor's sake.

This book is not designed to replace your family doctor, your chiropractor, your nutritionist, your therapist, your kindergarten teacher, your whoopee cushion, or your mom. It is not designed to replace personal pondering, prayer, or journaling. It is not designed to be an idol, American or otherwise, or to substitute for God.

By now, of course, you understand that Groveland Branch Press or the author have no responsibility or liability to anyone, anything, in any place, directly or indirectly, with regards to any damage or loss that may be blamed on this book. We love you just the same. If you must blame anyone for the mess you're in today, point the finger at that sinister circus clown who scared the cotton candy out of your hand onto your brand new Poll Parrot shoes.

If you cannot deal with the above in a binding way, you may return this book in perfect condition within 10 days, although that would make lots of people sad.

If you *can* deal with all this, read on, my understanding friend.

Introduction

We were so afraid of life, yet so bold. We were so loud, yet so shy. We took ourselves so seriously, yet we were so funny. We wanted respect, but we were so irreverent. We were so somber, yet so silly. We wanted to be wise, but we were so foolhardy. We were so daring, yet so cowardly. We were so smart, but so dumb.

We still are.

Our personal lockers are crammed full of important stuff, yet some days we can't even open our own combination locks.

And some days we bust a gasket, bent over peering into dark corners for stuff we don't remember cramming in.

We may have lost some memories, but we have gained lots of weight...er, wisdom. At this exciting time of Second Adulthood, a person who isn't expanding is...a person who isn't eating.

Are you about to abandon all the suffering and drama it's taken to get this far? Don't orphan your 16-year-old self. We *can* fuse past and present, just like the doctor fused your vertebrae after that vigorous ski trip in Canada, only with less pain.

We can't escape who we were. But don't be depressed. Who we are now is who we have always been, plus some insight...and lots more wrinkles.

Peek into my jumbled locker in the pages of this book. Compare my oddities with yours. I hope yours are odder. Valuables still lurk in dim corners. You might find something murky, yet familiar, that belongs to you. While you're in there, see if you can find my red licorice and Pizza Puffs—it's time for lunch.

BoomerTweeners™—you who feel too young to be old, too old to be young—this is the *worst* day of the rest of our lives! Wait...that's...the *first* day of the rest of our lives. See, we've found one of those valuables already!

And isn't that a Pizza Puff right over there? I'm bending, I'm breathing, getting closer, reaching, reaching, strrretching, it's kinda dusty...ow...ow...ouch.

There went my gasket.

Age is not important unless you are a cheese.
-Helen Hayes

Always leave your camping area cleaner than you found it.
-Eva Manwaring,
my girls camp director, 1970

The Sleep Of Hell
1971

My mother tried many times to kill me with her purple Hoover.

It was shaped like a pig. If I squinted, I saw a vicious purple swine on leash at her hand, straining to suck the breath out of me at the crack of noon on a Saturday morning, when all I wanted to do was sleep in just one more hour.

The old wives' tale of cats suffocating babies by stealing the breath from softly sleeping lips is a myth. In truth, it was my mother, her purple Hoover pig a tool in prying me out of bed on weekends, gulping all the fun and nourishment out of my deep growth sleep. How could anything grow under such hostile conditions? Perhaps that's why I remain flat-chested in my fifth decade of life.

She started cleaning the carpets at 10 a.m. every Saturday morning. I could sleep through it, even though our house was small. The huntress and her sidekick crawled through the house, mercifully saving my room for last. In between baking, mending, farm labor, and dusting, it took them until the inhuman hour of 11:30 a.m. to slurp dirt just beyond my door; her hunting pig gently but repeatedly bumping his snout against my wooden barrier.

Like a French porker hunting truffles she dogged me, until I lost all dreamy tentacles of sleep. Misty tendrils fled from the nightmarish gruntings at my hidden place...drowsy visions in teenage slumber.

Thus tiptoed in a denouement to my dreams; vacuumed up, ransacked by the out-of-control hog in her hand, leaving yawning holes of inconclusion—cliff-hangers of teenage castles in the sky, under siege by a wild boar.

Whack, whack. *Awake and arise from the dust, little girl.* Whack, whack, whack against my nerves. *Come, and **make** your dreams live. Come,* thump, *and,* thump, *be productive,* thump. *Come,* smack, smack, *and weed the beans.*

I could not reach the plug to kill the purple pig—not without getting up.

A vacuum in my heart and morning breath at noon. It was not pretty.

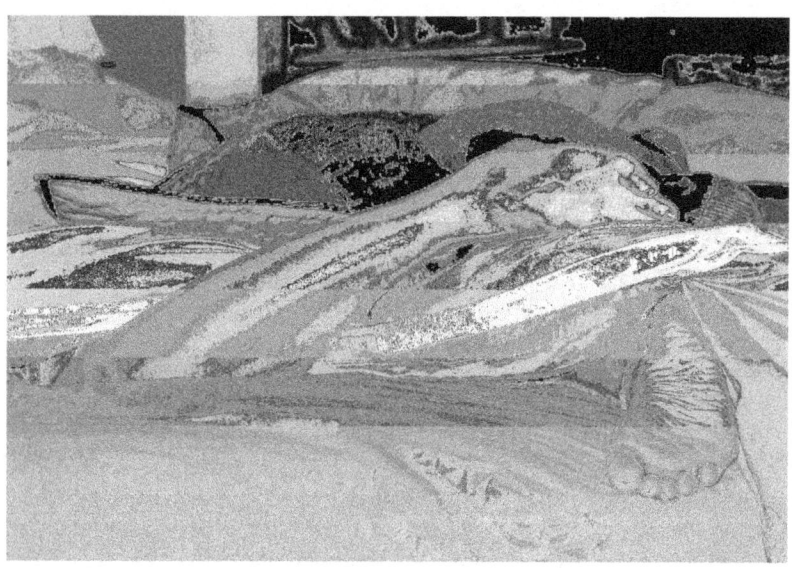

Stiff Competition
1972

  Way up in the nosebleed section of Idaho State University's Minidome, we *BroncCadettes*, the small and meek drill team from Blackfoot High School, stood with bated breath as the Pocatello High School Chiefettes (never call them Squaws) finished their polished performance. Way down below on an unnaturally green field (wow! a fake lawn the groundskeepers never have to mow, water, weed, or seed—hard, tough, and prickly—the first to sprout in America!) the Chiefettes stomped onto their hometown turf.

  The big-city girls from Poky were perfect. Toes pointed, arms straight, every thigh the same length, just like the Rockettes in New York City. Every leg was evenly bronzed, too—well, peached—with "California Coast Leg Tanning Foam." You couldn't see spotty streaks on calves from way up here. Using fakey foam coloring from a squirt can was much more *exotic* and beneficial than wearing pantyhose from J.C. Penney's. Flawless application made their kicks higher than ours. Enhanced, quality kicks.

  Creating tan legs from a squirt can was like frosting a warm twenty-four-layer cake with Cheez Whiz. To avoid streaks, you shook the can with passion and then hurried to smear wildly in a slow, careful way. Spots appeared like magic when the froth took an intense liking to one particular place on your leg. Achieving streaks and spots was easy. And then you looked like the Appaloosas and Pintos real chiefs used to ride.

  Pinto legs were much more *exotic*, but no more modest, than naked legs and those little elastic Greenies we wore. We hardly counted Greenies as cover-up, since they were basically heavy-duty stretchy granny underpants died to match the color of our uniforms. We liked to pretend that foam would defend as well as pantyhose from rug burns on turf. We also liked to pretend it gave us a layer of protection against the crowd of rude football boys who noticed when we weren't wearing nylons—heart burns from hard insults thrown at our thighs.

For a couple years, creamed legs were the latest trend in our personal luxury, even though their original chicness occurred twenty years earlier in San Francisco or some other *exotic* place. That's how long it took the latest fads to hit Blackfoot, Ideeho.

Seductive advertising on a can of fluff always suckered the BroncCadette's Dress Mistress and she'd rush into the locker room with the latest goo. "Hey, you guys, I've found a better brand. Listen! *'The Best Way to Bronze! New Liquid Foam from the California Coast—a new feel—a new wave—as refreshing as the ocean and as gentle as milk—California's scientifically complex formula brushes on skin like a sigh with fingertips for a startlingly natural-looking tan every time.'* Let's try it for Homecoming halftime!" She should have been a sales rep for California Coast. Maybe she was. We sure were seduced and we sure were startled. Our friends were, too. We heard those mocking yells from our own home stands: "Look at the orange zebras! Eewww! Diseased!"

We fixated on this one fact: you can't snag runs on creamed legs. Plus, streaky peach baby fat always seemed to look better than plain lily-white baby fat blubbering along with you. Yes, that orangey glow was certain defense against screamed catcalls from the sidelines, against nylon runs, against twenty-four colors of pantyhose purchased by a plethora of helpful moms. A rainbow of nylon tans with runs would instantly put you in the category of...small town. Some girl would bring Control Top Control Thigh nylons for a basketball halftime without checking them first to see what mom found at Kesler's Market on her quick stop to buy Spudnuts and dog food. No one ever had a spare pair to share with this unfortunate girl, except the lunch ladies. So during our halftime routine the Control Thigh peeked out like a gray girdle hanging down below her short flared skirt, and she would look like Grandma Grunt doing the boogaloo on the basketball court.

Since most all foams promising "bronze" ended up as peach, there were fewer style faux pas when frothy promises went awry. Everyone was equally glowing the same orange stain.

No Bare Beige, Sandy Beige, Ivory Beige, Almost Beige, Half-Hearted Beige, Nude Toe, Control Top, Girdle Hanging confusion here. All forty-eight kneecaps simply ended up beachy peach. Peaches from the beach, and what looked like grains of sand, that were, in reality, goose bumps. Unfortunately, spume coverage was no defense against the frigid air-conditioning in the Minidome or, as much as we hoped, no defense from rug burns as we executed splits on football turf.

The palms of Mrs. Peterson, our adviser and everyone's favorite English teacher, were often beachy peach, too. Someone had to apply it evenly, for quality control is sought in small towns just as it is in the big city. However, (and these were the suds that coagulated on the camel's back) Mr. Peterson didn't care much for beachy peach palms on Mrs. Peterson for nine months of a school year. Some strange hiccup in California Coast Leg Tanning Foam stained adult palms more severely than it did the frisky calves of youth.

Talk about severe—from toe to top the Pocatello girls were the stuff drill dreams are made of. Even every hair on their heads was in place as fifty—count 'em!—fifty heads snapped to the left in unison as the Poky dancers pivoted perfectly around the six shortest girls on their squad. They were floating around in that formation like tale hair on a barrel racer's Quarter horse.

We BroncCadettes only had twenty-four girls in our ranks and, since Pam was sick, we had no choice but to cut Debbie out of the competition routine, too. You can't make quality formations with odd numbers. Unlike the principles of home decorating, drill teams need even numbers for fancy formations. Bad luck when your partner is upchucking back home in Blackfoot. Pam had food poisoning from El Mariachi's El Grande Burrito. We strongly cautioned our girls: *when you're in competition, burritos weaken legs and stomachs, and drinking two Swamp Waters along with Combination Plate #6 is dancing suicide.* To make Swamp Water you must use equal parts root beer and orange soda pop, then float three crispy dill pickle slices on top. Like slurping lily pads and the irrigation pond on my family's farm, only yummier.

But here floated fifty sets of teased, sprayed, bobby-pinned curls atop fifty heads. Perky, helpful curls, Aqua Net-sprayed-heartily until those curls were forced to cooperate and couldn't possibly move against the flow of what wriggled on down below. Those fifty wads of curls were as precise as the girls marching underneath them.

Ah, wiglets, how we love you! You save the short-haired girls from feeling like rude football boys, stout, shaved, and sweaty, among a corps of dainty ballerinas. You save the long-haired girls from drooping. You save us all from imprecision and deunification. Wiglets, everready for action on the football field, as much a staple to drill teams as pantyhose. Or, leg foam.

The Chiefettes' song crescendoed now as "Proud Mary" came to a blaring close over the loudspeakers. In a single long chorus line, fifty girls leaped off the ground as one, facing their hometown crowd. Fifty right legs split high, higher, in the air, and came down hard in saucy splits. Every one of them split on the same lead leg. All twenty-two BroncCadettes gasped in unison. *Leaping* splits on tough, prickly turf. A new trick kicked in our faces!

Regrettably, three of the BroncCadettes had to split with their left legs poking out in front, when it is the right leg that all drill teams and competition judges embrace as the paradigm of perfection. Left legs were allowed at BHS. It was just the way it had to be in order to have twenty-four girls on the squad. There weren't any more girls at Blackfoot High who could do the splits on any leg.

Except Patty Parsons. But at lunchtime Patty Parsons liked to call other girls out to fight in the parking lot. One could *not* march on the same turf with Patty Parsons. One did not *walk* next to Patty Parsons at school. Patty could *spit* better than she could *split*.

Fifty big city girls held onto those splits without quivering and then, *then*, flopped forward over their fifty right legs poking out in front to *bow* to wild screaming adoration from the hometown crowd. Snap! Fifty heads shot back up historically. No, no, not a *new* variation on the *new* trick! We were glad their backs were to us. From our precarious perch in the nosebleed section we could only imagine the Vaseline gleaming on their big smiley teeth. There was more than one BroncCadette wanting to wipe fifty smiles off those fifty nemesis... nemeses... nemesissies... who beat us every time we faced them with Vaseline smiles on our own faces. Where was Patty Parsons when you needed her? Thankfully, "Proud Mary" was finished.

Twenty-two BroncCadettes groaned at that finale, at our stiff competition, turning away in dismay as the big city girls gracefully scooped themselves up out of the Leaping Bowing Turf Splits and smartly stepped off the floor in unison, heads held high.

"Oh, my heck," Mrs. Peterson stopped us. "Look!"

Something was different, something not so precise, something… had strayed. Count them—fifty girls with fifty curls. No, fifty girls with forty-nine curls. There was a little girl, who had a little curl…but she left it right in the middle of the Minidome.

Freed from the high pressure of competition, flung forward over a smooth, proud brow toward the hometown crowd, lying on the prickly turf like a naughty cockapoo…a wiglet sat. A clever wiglet sat so alone, waiting for its perky mistress to call it home for a biscuit.

It waited and waited.

The cockapoo's mistress never called it home. She was too frantic, scrambling toward the outer limits of Parking Lot K, running to her blue Gremlin before anyone could point fingers or see her tears.

There are blessings aplenty for small town girls, dressed simply in kelly-green, in peachy foam *or* pantyhose, in plain ponytails, and in hope springing eternal.

There are blessings from heaven for Mini-dome groundskeepers of newfangled turf, willing to scoop up behind rude football players, an occasional galloping rodeo queen and her pony, and other high-stepping creatures.

Perfection became a myth at the same moment that history was made.

For on that very day, twenty-two BroncCadettes kicked up their heels and, dancing into history, trotted home with their first trophy.

They also brought home a very quiet little cockapoo nicknamed Naughty Poky—a special gift from a charming groundskeeper living in the big city of Pocatello, who, thirty-four years earlier, was a small, rude football boy. A mighty Bronco from Blackfoot High, he once enjoyed catcalling and whistling at his own high-stepping pals, choosing no better way to express public appreciation of his female friends than being tough and prickly. Until now.

Naughty Poky took up permanent residence inside her new gold cup, at home in the main hall trophy case at BHS. She lies there snug and safe to this very day, happy in retirement, dreaming vivid, marvelous memories of her adoptive team's victory.

Put your ear to the glass and she'll whisper the true tale of triumph that arrived only after snags, streaks, and struggles. Though fun it is to divulge dance stories, her best delight is to reveal the tender secret hearts, long hidden, of rude football boys.

My Email Audition
2003

----- Original Message -----
From: pict
To: academyawardmama
Sent: Thursday, January 09, 2003 1:55 p.m.
Subject: Please audition!

    Yes, New Grandma I want to see you audition! Every character in the chorus is a real character. As the director I want to get to know you as a performer.
My Best...Cecil

----- Reply -----
From: academyawardmama
To: pict
Sent: Friday, January 10, 2003 10:19 a.m.
Subject: Email audition!

Dear Cecil,

    I had a feeling I would miss the auditions Monday night and sure enough, I did. My gorgeous granddaughter fooled us all by coming six days early. So I thought, well, while I'm here explaining why I missed auditions, I will just audition for you by email. So here goes. I wonder if Meryl Streep ever had to endure such conditions.
    First my solo. I have chosen to sing for you a peppy little number I wrote myself many years ago (but it seems like just

yesterday) when I played with a group of girls from my high school called The Pea Pickers. (Oh, my high school was not called The Pea Pickers, my girlfriends were, although it was not peas we picked, it was potatoes.) It is called "Shafted." I am accompanying myself on my guitar. Just a minute while I fix this pesky G string. (The G string on the guitar. I am actually wearing the black tights I rehearsed in for *Carousel,* with a filmy black chiffon overskirt so I can move properly during the dance portion of my audition; over a black leo that I haven't washed since *Carousel* rehearsals. But this is not aromatherapy, it is an audition.)

OK, I'm ready. I am not *miked.* (If I spell it *miced* it seems like I am being attacked by rodents. I am not.) I don't have a *mic,* so listen carefully.

> "S is for the stinkin' way you treated me.
> H is for the heartache you instilled in me.
> A is for the animal you turned out to be.
> F is for you, fink, I never had you anyway.
> T is for the times that you lied to me.
> E is for every time you set me free.
> D is for the dirty rotten, low down, gall-durn, snake-in-the-grass you wuz. And that's what shafted means."

I would continue, but I've probably exceeded my time limit already on the singing portion; and since high school was a long time ago even though it seems like just yesterday, I'm not sure I can remember the rest of the six verses, and I'm sure by now you appreciated the high C and the low F I hit, as well as the fairly even vibrato on the long, drawn out notes. I hope you didn't notice how my nails scratched the neck of my guitar on that last riff. Ooooh, it's like a chalkboard scratch and would've made you pucker.

Talk about pucker…I apologize for my dry mouth. I'm always a little nervous at auditions. But remember, the Bible says: "If ye are prepared ye will not fear." I wonder if Moses ever got dry mouth. Maybe Charlton Heston would know.

Now for the dancing. I'm going to put on my black ballet slippers while my tape is fast forwarding to the right spot—just so I don't waste your time. There. No. Back a little. Sorry, I just hit the fast forward button instead of rewind. Why? Oh, my heck, I'm shaking. It must be adrenalin, it couldn't be stage fright! OK, OK. Here we are. I know you will appreciate Judy Garland's rendition of "Happy Days" while I do the routine from *Carousel* that we did in front of Aunt What's-Her-Name's house...sorry there are no new steps here, sorry I don't have *Carousel* music, and sorry that I can't remember the aunty character played by Jackie, but I've been so busy and distracted lately. Lucy's in heat (my Jack Russell terrier) and I have to protect her from our neighbor's dog Shelby's little mutty friend down the street. You may not know what *little* willpower terriers have when it comes to socializing. Shelby is female, but her mutty friend is not, and he has been coming over for a peek and a sniff way too often lately without properly introducing himself. As soon as this audition is over I'm getting out my slingshot and scrounging some marbles from our board game of *Aggravation*; oh, yes, and all the colorful pointy pieces from *Sorry*.

OK, so sit back and relax and just enjoy this.

********** ********** **********

Phew! I didn't realize how tricky that last gymnastic-type maneuver would be without Andrea Wixom's back to jump on...but did you appreciate how high my hitch kick was today?

You know what really ticked me off? It was watching the video recording of our *Carousel* and realizing that Sasha or Vladimir or whoever it was who *professionally* taped our *Carousel* totally MISSED my hitch kick coming off the dock ramp. Well, that's show biz for ya. But now you know why I didn't order a copy of our show. And he wanted $20 a tape, for Pete's sake!

OK. Now I will do my character reading. Since I don't have the script for your new show *Bye Bye Birdie* here at home in my old book of plays we used in high school, and so cannot possibly assume any characters you're looking for, I shall portray the character Mrs. Stevenson from Lucille Fletcher's one act play *Sorry, Wrong Number*. Cold. I have never been in this play before. (And I give Lucille all the credit. You have to credit these writer-types since they're pretty touchy about *every* word they put down on paper.) I realize it's not in the same genre as *Birdie*, but I promise you, I will emote. It will be just as intense as anything you've seen so far. Here we go. Oh, since I'm here alone, I shall play all the parts. That will allow you to see my full range. It's important for an actress to evoke, I know.

OK, here we go. I still have a little dry mouth...let me just take a tiny sip of Tang. Mmmm, OK, aaahhemmm...OK...
"MRS. STEVENSON: That-that click just now – in my own telephone? As though someone had lifted the receiver off the hook of the extension phone downstairs -
WOMAN: I hear it, Madam, now about this -
MRS. STEVENSON: (Scared): But I did. There's someone in this house. Someone downstairs in the kitten. And they're listening to me now. They're – (Hangs up phone. In a suffocated voice.) I won't pick it up. I won't let them hear me. I'll be quiet – and they'll think – (With growing terror.) But if I don't call someone now – while they're still down there – there'll be no time. (She picks up the receiver. Bland buzzing signal. She dials operator. Rings twice.)
OPERATOR: (Fat and lethargic): Your call, please?
MRS. STEVENSON: (a desperate whisper) Operator, I-I'm in desperate trouble – I -
OPERATOR: I cannot hear you, madam. Please speak louder.
MRS. STEVENSON: (still whispering): I don't dare. I – there's someone listening. Can you hear me now?
OPERATOR: Your call, please? What number are you calling, madam?
MRS. STEVENSON: (desperately) You've got to hear me. Oh, please. You've got to help me. There's someone in this house. Someone who's going to murder me. And you've got to get in touch with the – (Click of receiver being put down in Mrs. Stevenson's line. Bursting out wildly.) Oh, there it is – he's put it down – he's put down the extension – he's coming – (She screams) He's coming up the stairs – (hoarsely) Give me the Police Department – (screaming) the police!
OPERATOR: Ringing the police department.
(Phone is rung. We hear sound of a train beginning to fade in. On second ring, Mrs. Stevenson screams again, but roaring of train drowns out her voice. For a few seconds we hear nothing but roaring of train, then dying away, phone at police headquarters ringing.)
FLUFFY: Police Department. Precinct 43. Fluffy speaking. (pause) Police Department. Fluffy speaking.
GEORGE: Sorry. Wrong number. (Hangs up.)"

    Wow, I don't know about you, but I have chills. Wait a minute. I have to run and lock my doors and yank the drapes and grab the toilet plunger just in case I have to whack someone. I am not taking time to pull out the slingshot right now or find my marbles.

OK, I'm back. I do apologize though. In being fully developed as a character, I inadvertently...in my terrorized excitement...said 'kitten' instead of 'kitchen.' Of course, no one's in the *kitten*, it would be in the kitchen. How ridiculous would that be for some terrorized woman to be in a *kitten*? Now she might be *having* a cow, but not even then would she be *in* a cow. Which is nothing like the Old Woman who lived in a shoe, not a cow. Or the Old Lady who swallowed a fly, not a cow or a kitten. Boy, people sure insult old women, don't they? Mrs. Stevenson wasn't old, she was terrorized. So, how ridiculous...oh, but I digress. Where was I? Oh...we were having cows, but not in a cow, oh yes...and some terrorized woman *in* a kitten. She would be *having* a *kitten* and how bad would that be, really, to have a kitten? I've had four children and let me tell you, it would be a picnic to have a kitten. Sorry, I digress again.

Oh, but after I got so terrified...I became FLUFFY! Being the professional you are, you know it's supposed to be DUFFY. Have you ever heard of a cop named *Fluffy*? I don't think so. Well, because of donuts, I guess, they become fluffy, but people only call them that behind their backs. So, I kind of blew that character's name, although I *was* in the moment. My typing fingers were, too. I scare myself. You'll just have to trust me. Oh, and one more thing: I apologize for not having a real train roaring through my house. Humming harshly on the kazoo is just not the same, but I hope you got the picture.

Well, there you have it. I do appreciate your kind scrutiny of my talents and thank you for your kind attention and for letting me audition over the Internet. I wonder if Meryl Streep ever performed such an email audition. I bet not. I'm sure she never auditions anymore. People just *want* her. They *clamor* for her.

I don't know about you, but this was a first for me. I'm glad we could share this memorable moment together. Hey, let's do lunch! In honor of your upcoming musical, we will eat a chicken, yes, a fried chicken! Okey-dokey, I hope *Bye Bye Birdie* makes all your dreams come true and that everyone breaks their legs.
XOXOXOX New Granny J

Actress's Note: This audition must have made some impression, although I was not assigned a part, not even a chorus part, in *Birdie*... (But then, neither was Miss Meryl Streep.) (Let's blame it on my new granddaughter.) I *was* offered a chance to audition for a future starring role...if we ever do...*Sorry, Wrong Number*! Perhaps as Fluffy.

Publisher's Note:
My Email Audition was the 1st prize winner in the Adult Fiction category of the 2003 San Juan County Fair, wherein Ms. Oliver was awarded a blue ribbon and a cash prize sufficient to buy two corn dogs and one fresh-squeezed lemonade...a wild celebration.

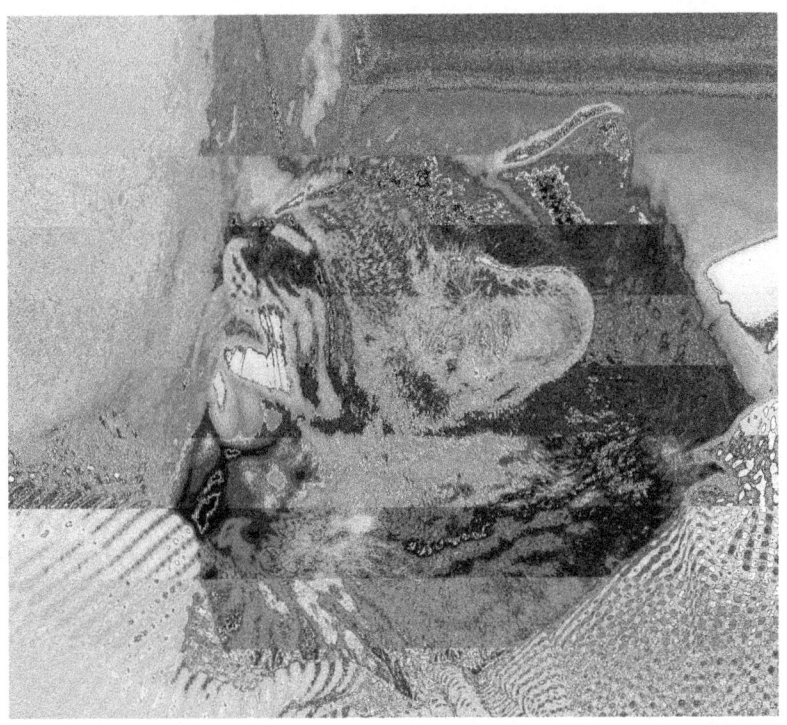

Well done is better than well said.
- Benjamin Franklin

George Gray

I have studied many times
The marble which was chiseled for me—
A boat with a furled sail at rest in a harbor.
In truth it pictures not my destination
But my life.
For love was offered me
And I shrank from its disillusionment;
Sorrow knocked at my door, but I was afraid;
Ambition called to me, but I dreaded the chances.
Yet all the while I hungered for meaning in my life.
And now I know that we must lift the sail
And catch the winds of destiny
Wherever they drive the boat.
To put meaning in one's life may end in madness,
But life without meaning is the torture
Of restlessness and vague desire—
It is a boat longing for the sea and yet afraid.

-Edgar Lee Masters
Spoon River Anthology

Country Road Take Me Home
1988

What doesn't kill you will make the back of your knees swell up.

In May it's a tradition among our church group to experience the "50/20" Hike. This is a grueling little stroll of fifty miles that must be finished in twenty hours. Dang that Amos Alonzo Stagg.

He's the original fool who motivated this thing; some kind of sporty guy, some grand old man of football who coached for a hundred years or so. My nine-year-old daughter made it thirty miles last year without our help, so I volunteered to walk with her this year to see if we can both make it. Erin wants to wear the real Alonzo Stagg gold medal around her neck for finishing this hike.

All of us start at 3:00 a.m. on a dark May morning fifty miles south of home in the boonies and must make it to the church parking lot by 11 p.m. We walk fast. I walk with my teen friends—girls I teach at church and supervise at Girls Camp. We giggle and push each other and skip along the first five miles. Suddenly I know why we start out in the dark, as Erin and I veer off into the peach orchard. Luckily I've brought my own toilet paper. I really like doing my morning constitutional behind the six inch diameter of an Early Elberta peach trunk. Don't stop again to smell the roses. If you do, you'll stiffen up, and that is death on this trek. Prior Preparation Prevents Poor Performance, the old-timers warned us.

Ten miles and I'm still feeling good, although I notice that my daughter and teen friends are up ahead of me about a quarter mile and I'm now walking with women my age. The sun is shining, the seagulls yell encouragement. All is well in farm country.

My husband Steve, and his support guys drive by in our van with Gatorade and granola bars. I have some. Carefully. Knowing there aren't many peach orchards up ahead.

Twenty miles down and I'm feeling the pebbles on the bottom of my shoes. I'm walking alone. The sophomore boys on the cross-country team have walked a mile, run a mile. It's 10:30 a.m. and they are already home. Bratty little underachievers.

By thirty miles I'm putting one foot in front of another. Our people are strung out within a ten mile range of each other. Steve's turned our van over to two teenage boys and dubbed them Car Support Guys so he can keep me company. I see the little country store up ahead where the non-running-normal-walking kids have made a pit stop. Chocolate milk. A real bathroom. A huge mistake. I'm so stiff after my break I have to take Steve's hands and let him pull me up. The Store Guy asks, "Why d'you people come by here every year? Jist can't figger it out. Ya torture yerselves and fer what? Doncha know when to quit?" He was glaring at me.

"Because it's a test of courage...of endurance...?" I murmur feebly. *Because of the foolish traditions of our fathers?* I ask myself. Because who wants to be the wuss to put a stop to it?

After thirty-one miles I feel two barn rats attached to the back of my knees. No, no, they are coyotes...no...make that hogs. Yes, two farm hogs the size of hippos have dug their tusks into the back of my knees and I am dragging them down this lane. Country road take me home to the place I belong—my bubble bath, my bed.

I shuffle down the middle of the road because I can now feel every grain of sand under my soles and there seem to be fewer here. I'm tilting, and if I make the slightest wrong move I will lean right on over into the borrow pit full of irrigation water and become a piece of flotsam like the cigarette butts and cow pies floating along, gently bumping into each other. A farmer moseys by in an old brown Ford pick-up truck and waits patiently for me to move. I can't. He just eases around me, gives me that look that country folk give to city slickers. I know that look, 'cuz I used to be one and I used to give it.

I begin to cry and look over at Steve. "I'm sorry," I snivel.

"For what?" he asks.

"I don't know...I'm just sorry...for everything..." I sob as I plod along and when he puts his arm around my shoulders, I cry harder.

We see Erin up ahead and she is boobing a little bit, too. I dry my eyes as we shuffle up to her. "I don't know if I can make it," she cries.

Matt and Tim cruise by in our van, "You've gone thirty-nine miles! Keep up the good work! We'll wait for you at Burger King!" They zoom off. *Wait! Wait for me,* my mind whimpers.

We circle our wagons. My daughter and I cry forehead to forehead, our tears making polka dots on hot asphalt. "We can do it, Erin," I promise. "Let's think of Great-grandma Sarah." She nods, sniffling. We straighten our shoulders and Steve walks between us holding our hands. I'm dragging those hog hippos every step of the way.

Just before the forty-mile paradise of Burger King, I stop Erin, gripping her shoulders. We look at each other and begin sniffling again. It's time for my hardy pioneer-stock speech.

"Erin, think of yourself as a pioneer girl who must get to Salt Lake Valley," I whisper pitifully. She nods. "I'm your ma and I'm just not going to make it. I'm dying on the trail. Pa can either help you or me in, but not both of us, and since we don't have any other helpers who can drag me in, I want him to go with you. You can do it," I weep convincingly without even acting. She wails and hugs me and gets the picture. Steve stands steadfast. Oh, it's a poignant moment.

"Don't stop now. You keep right on going. You do it for both of us," I plead. "Just put a marker on my shallow grave right here," I gurgle threw my juicy face. Steve bends over, picks a dandelion from the shoulder of the road and tosses it on the tarmac at my feet.

"Okay, Mom, I will." She lets go of me and puts both arms around Steve's waist. He carries her like a barnacle on his left hip. Just a clammy little cocklebur in the arid wilderness.

Meanwhile, back in the prairie van, Ma has died and gone to heaven. Out of the Burger King parking lot Matty Lou drives us because I can no longer bend my knees. We pass Erin and Steve three miles from the Promised Land. We honk and wave and shout encouragement. "Forty-seven miles – only three more to go!" The Desert Barnacle is still stuck on his hip and doesn't look up. Steve is still just rolling along like a tumblin' tumble weed.

At the church, Matty Lou and Timmy haul me out of the van. I crawl over to the sign-in board and put a big "40 miles" next to my name. I wait and wait for my daughter and my husband, our support man who has walked almost as many miles as the rest of us. My Prairie Girl finally makes it in, lurching at a painful trot on her own two legs the last fifty yards, whooping as she signs in at 6:30 p.m.

She gets her medal in church the next day and wears it proudly. I'm busting buttons even without a medal because I hobbled in at forty miles.

I started out prancing fast and giddy with teen girls, the party I thought I could travel with, and that hopeful enthusiasm took me quite a ways down my country road. But when surprising critters attached themselves to me with a new kind of pain, my learnin' came hard and fast.

Sometimes the finish you expect becomes a mirage. Sometimes your pardners on the trail evolve from being your sidekicks to becoming your heroes and *you* turn out to be the sidekick. Sometimes, as you blaze your own pioneer trail, the expected pace doesn't matter one whit, as long as you stagger, crawl, or are carried in, alive and feebly kickin'.

Sometimes sacrifice hurts really good...because it renews the spirit more completely than accomplishment can.

If *you* aren't willing to sacrifice for your child, who is? Because always, at the end of the trek, what's really fine is watching your young 'un finish on her own two feet—even if it's in a painful, limpy sprint.

Three days later Erin is skipping around and flipping cartwheels. It takes three weeks before the hog hippos reluctantly drop off my legs and go back to the jungle. The back of my knees stay swollen and I can't walk right for three months.

Amos Alonzo Stagg, wherever you are, go take a hike!

A bend in the road is not the end of the road...unless you fail to make the turn.

-Author Unknown

"Sorry don't get it done, Dude."
-John T. (John Wayne)
in *Rio Bravo*

The business of living is not to get ahead of others but to get ahead of ourselves.
-Author Unknown

Much of the language we have inherited about religious experience speaks of sacrifice as though it were a way of erasing yourself, a way of erasing your own value or the value of your desires. ...Sacrifice is giving up something you want very much for something you want more.
-Francine R. Bennion

I've Been 16 for 34 Years - BoomerTweener

PMS—The Not-So-Pretty Picture Book
1993

Mother feels like getting up in the morning. She feels like getting dressed. She feels like loving everyone.

Mother tries to share her innermost thoughts with her children. They look at her strangely and slowly edge away. That's OK. She still values her innermost thoughts.

Mother volunteers at Mark's elementary school. See how the children love her as they learn how to hand-quilt pot holders for the social studies unit on pioneers. Then Mother is off for a brisk walk to admire nature, tone her muscles, energize her mind, and clean out her heart.

Mother sews a ballet skirt for her teenage daughter in order to beat the exorbitant retail price of this little piece of chiffon sold in the dance shop. Will Erin wear it? No. It looks stupid. Will she try it on? No. It does not look exactly like every other ballet skirt in her dance class.

Mother sews a second ballet skirt for her teenage daughter, all the while smiling, smiling, happy to share her domestic heritage with the next generation. Will Erin wear it? Yes! Mother was clever in creating the next new original pattern based on the shape of the toilet seat in the downstairs bathroom. Sometimes it takes safely stooping a little lower than usual to get a smile from a teen. Mother and daughter share silver laughter at her cleverness.

Mother volunteers at K.C.'s middle school on Job Fair Day. See how the children love her as she shares secrets of the business world and bread and cookies from her bakery? They smack their lips and are satisfied.

Father and Mother share a romantic interlude alone on a Friday night. They work hard to date every week to keep their marriage perky. They overeat at Cucina! Cucina! They watch the movie *Waterworld* and weep at the millions overspent. Later, they even play Tickle Buns. These buns are not sold in their bakery. They smack lips and are satisfied.

Mother volunteers at Nick and Erin's high school with extreme caution. She is careful not to embarrass her teens. She tries to wear the right clothes and say the right things. Many other teens smile and talk to her. Her own children smile guardedly and talk shortly to her and move away quickly. That's OK. Mother remembers what it was like to have her own mother among her peers. Ooohhhh, scary.

Father and Mother sit on the back porch in the afternoon sun and discuss *The Trial By Existence* by Robert Frost. They share a warm bonding moment with little sparrows twittering in the background. Mother cooks an interesting new dish for dinner. It contains no meat, just fresh colorful veggies. She hums a tune while preparing the evening meal. She is included in the family's happy chatter. After grace is said they devour her tasty offering and then some of them burp. Pardon! The whole family laughs.

Then...oh, my...Mother begins to ovulate. How does she know this without peeking into a microscope? She is proud to know her own body after so many years. She knows what those achy female body parts mean fourteen days after her last Monthly Visitor. Fifth-Grade Maturation Clinic didn't tell the whole truth. Mother is hungry for popcorn and chocolate.

See Mother run! See how she multitasks! Mother can do many chores at the same time that she ovulates. Mother must do lots of chauffeuring today for her children: dance lessons, karate lessons, and baseball practice. She is ready to give a long, loud primal scream in traffic. She chooses not to frighten her children.

Mother forgets several important appointments today. That's OK. She needed some quiet time alone before traffic.

Mother wishes she had a personal trainer to help her through the next two weeks—to cook her tasty food without fat, sugar, salt, or preservatives; to lead her in yoga and semi-aerobic exercise; to massage her achy muscles; to protect her from the loud demands of her world. Oh! Oh! See? And to be her body double!

Mother soaks in her hot bubble bath so long that the scalding water turns warm, the bubbles melt away, and her family all goes to bed. She can come out now.

How many pounds has she gained overnight? Fifty? Take a tiny peek at the scales and see. Just three? So it's not all in her head! Will Mother fit into her pants today? Oh, happy day, she fits into her fat pants. Yikes! They are tight. Her skinny pants will have to wait a couple weeks. Maybe she could invent a handy shoe horn for pant zippers. Yes, a pant-horn!

Suddenly Mother becomes enraged at the toenail clippings Father left in the bathroom sink. Four days ago they only bothered her a teensy bit. Mother has been patiently waiting and pondering, *What do toenails in the sink mean and why has he clipped them there?* Four days ago she might have said to Father, "Oh, how cute and romantic, to leave a part of you as a souvenir for me while you go off to work." She is not saying that now.

For dinner tonight Mother struggles to make a big pot of Minute Rice. Somewhere in the recesses of her memory she knows no one complains about eating rice. Complaints might make her want to break the big picture window in the living room. She sets the pot of rice down in the middle of the table so all can feast upon it. Whack! Ooooops, it comes down harder than she intends it to. Only twelve grains of rice leap from the pot, escaping their iron prison. A pregnant pause of silence. Her family looks up at her in wonder. Father rises to get the butter and salt and pepper. Yum, grains for dinner. Just pure white grains. Eat up, children. They do. With no burping. With no laughter.

After dinner Mother hears a loud whining voice. Oh dear! It is coming from her mouth? Her family is wincing. That is not OK. She sends herself to her room. Who is that stranger staring at her from the mirror? She wishes she had made several special signs for such a time as this. Like:

HELP

ME!!

RALLY ROUND!

I'M STUCK!!

HUG ME

NOW!!

Finally, Mother's Monthly Visitor is here. What a relief. Five special days.

Day One. Mother has learned to pamper herself with this recipe: two Motrin plus two Midol every four hours. This keeps her alive. She didn't learn that in Fifth-Grade Maturation Clinic. She discovered it for herself just two short years ago. Mother wants to throw a brick through the TV screen at the feminine hygiene ads. Instead, she will eat popcorn and chocolate.

Day Two. Her crotch wants to fall off. She knows this pain is only temporary. She hopes that someday scientists will have a special name for it, and a special cure.

Day Three. Aaaaahhhh, the killer cramps are gone. Just a few twinges left. Mother can walk and talk again like a normal person. She is calm. Father is calm. Her children are calm.

Day Four. She goes for a slow walk in semi-skinny pants to return to nature, rejuvenate her muscles, recover her mind, and retrieve her heart. Smile. Eat. Hug the children. Really hug Father.

Day Five. Be happy. Make rice with lots of other food stuffs and Twinkies for dessert. Yay! Mother burps first and others follow loudly. Pardon! The whole family laughs.

Mother feels like getting up this morning. She feels like getting dressed. She feels like loving everyone.

The End
(Not)

Oh! See! See! The miraculous cycle of life. Stop! Look! Listen! Forgive! The family must pardon when the family burps. Relieve the painful gas.

If you can't be a good example then you'll just have to be a horrible warning.
-Catherine Aird

I wear the chain I forged in life. I made it, link by link, and yard by yard.
–Charles Dickens
Jacob Marley, in
A Christmas Carol

There are two freedoms: The false, where a man is free to do what he likes; the true, where a man is free to do what he ought.
- Charles Kingsley

The Terrible Horrible Tinkley Gangrenous Day
(in two parts)
1995

Part 1

There is some happy stuff in this world that just makes you sick.

Steve plays softball with a bunch of guys who are 16 in their hearts and 24+ years in their limbs and torsos. Naturally then, they play injured. Hamstring pulls are the most common objection to their sporadic vigor. These absurdities happen often, easily.

On one game night in July, Steve fielded all fly balls, had no errors, hit two solid doubles, and let his bat and glove do his talking to our undefeated opponents, even in the face of some bizarre pressure.

The opposing pitcher had a fat belly and a fat ego. Don't ya just know he played high school baseball. Or maybe he never made the team. Naturally then, in his little mind he was a New York Yankee. Yes, a way overly dramatic one of those. You know the type. A wannabe with Dunlap's Disease—his belly done lapped over his belt—and tragically, his mind done lapped over, too.

If there is anything more unattractive than that, kindly let me know.

My back was turned from the excitement on the field for one wee moment—only just as Steve cracked a Hit of Great Consequence off Mr. Dunlap. Where was I? Busy in our Right Fielder's eyebrow, swabbing out his cut. He'd snagged a zinging low fly ball with his forehead, and wobbled so bad that, unlike a Weeble, he *did* fall down. On his face. He broke his

Crown; so let's call him Jack. Rather than the ball, Jack's left *cheek* dropped into his empty glove as he hit the dirt. But only his wife, Jill, was happy about his cheek. The ball ricocheted off to center field after a quick stop at our teammate's temple.

When Jack arose from his episode on the ground, he became a teensy bit hysterical. He wobbled directly to the dugout as his gooey eye observed that his teammates on the field were ignoring his boo-boo. As our benchwarmers screamed for the third out, he wisely bypassed them and teetered up into the stands to Jill for some TLC. Since *she* couldn't deal with his blood she became infected with his frenzy; so Jack and Jill looked at *me* to take over the decontamination event.

I dabbed at it with a hydrogen peroxide soaked cotton ball in a gentle sort of way while he trembled and winced. (*Not* like Meryl Streep's scene in *Silkwood* where six yellow-plastic-coated detoxifiers scrub her frantically with honkin' big brillo pads on sticks.) I softly murmured to Jack that my butterfly bandage would stop his blood flow and leave no scars, and that frantic Jill didn't need to rush him or his petite cut to the ER. (Take note of this symbolic foreshadowing of my near future.) Jack resisted my soothing ways, thus forcing me into firmer murmurings. I was totally distracted when s*omeone* connected with a loud crack of the bat.

I turned in time to see Steve already running to second base. My but he was moving fast. *My husband was fleeing from what some thought inevitable.* The enemy's young Center Fielder sprinted hard to catch this humongous hit, but I was much more impressed with how *fast* Steve was running. He wanted a home run ba-aad. I couldn't believe how *fast* he was running. The ball dropped smack at the back fence. My bones knew that Steve had an in-park home run made in the shade of that big oak tree just beyond the fence. He was running so fast I couldn't believe it. The Fielder dug for the ball, spun around, and heaved it hard.

Steve checked his stride for a nanosecond as he was rounding third; a brief stutter step that told me something was wrong. He had hurt himself. He drove hard for home, undaunted by pain. Our fans in the stands held their collective breath. The cotton ball dripped in my hand. Jack and Jill stopped twitching. The hydrogen peroxide, marbled pink with his blood, dribbled down Jack's face as he watched this glorious spectacle.

My husband was fleeing. From the ball, from the pain, from something invisible chasing him down from behind. I felt what it was but couldn't bear to think it.

Ten feet from home plate, Steve put on that *face*. I recognized that grimace. It's the contortion he always wears just before he starts his slide. Don't tell me men don't know how to accessorize. Whenever Steve dresses for success with this scowl, he's never tagged out.

Wickedly, like a city gal at a Nordstrom One-Day Shoe Sale, Mr. Dunlap leaped in from the pitcher's mound, blocking home plate, his glove dangling empty under his belly. In classic trauma slow-motion style, he shouldered my man, knocking him flat on his back, stripping the success scowl from Steve's face. That over inflated tube sock of a pitcher didn't even possess the ball. The Shortstop had the ball. He fired it at Mr. Dunlap as Steve thumped backwards in the dirt.

Like a true champ, Steve ignored this new pain and scurried inch by inch, heels first, hands following, to home plate. Even in my anguish for him, I couldn't help but notice he looked very crab-like in his scrabble. Crab, one of my favorite things to eat, had now become my husband.

Crusty and unpretentious, season after season he denied himself the purchase of a real pair of baseball pants with padding in the knees because we had four children who needed to wear pants and kept outgrowing their own. They just couldn't help it. After ruining six different pairs of jeans by sliding into home on his left knee, I strongly suggested he either buy padding, let me swaddle him with an old grandma quilt, or wear his holey jeans forevermore when playing baseball. So, he started every game with a giant raggedy hole from whence his gooey left knee peeked out of its denim window shouting, "Scab me! Scab me more!"

His sliding knee, skinned all summer long, went unprotected all summer long. He scored points with goo in his knee and grit in his teeth.

At this moment I was most tender toward his left knee, wriggling out of its peek hole just above the dust. My beloved plucky crab, in holey pants and a big old scab, was on the ground, scuttling. He got game.

He got game alright—touching home with his heel just before Mr. Dunlap tagged him. Steve laid there wrecked, like a prize catch from the deep blue sea, as his teammates ran over to collect the flotsam. I ached for him in this holy moment. I wanted to scoop him up to apply a kiss and a mighty dose of hydrogen peroxide.

In the third inning we had witnessed Mr. Dunlap attack our second baseman, Chris, the same way—very deliberate, very cruel—especially to olding farts wearing various strains and sprains and holey items. But this sport-thug wasn't even thrown out of the game.

I forgot all about being Florence Nightingale, forsook my gentle murmurings, my calm cotton ball ministrations, and exclaimed loudly as I stomped down the bleachers, flexing my long, strong fingernails, "I'm going down there to scratch his eyes out."

"He's just a jerk. It won't be worth it," grumbled Phil, our catcher. I was unconvinced.

What is it about a simple, happy, friendly game that can cause such an outpouring of ugly?

Instead of physically reacting as I preferred, I trapped myself behind the backstop, gripped the wire mesh and yelled, "Bush league! Throw him out of the game!" They didn't.

Even with Steve's spectacular play we lost by one point. "That loss hurt more than anything," he said. I was unconvinced. I had experienced vibes of his earlier personal nano-second of injury.

As he rounded third base, Steve heard something snap inside his leg. His teammates heard it, too. He cracked, scrambled, shattered or popped something in his right calf. All the way home from the ballpark he was in pain, but refused to go see a doctor because we were still paying off the Visa card, Children's Hospital for K.C.'s liver disease and his braces, Nick's Summer Scholar's Academy, Erin's dance lessons, Mark's shoes, and saving for four sets of upcoming school fees and pants. It will heal just fine without a doctor's help, like your sprained MCL did months ago, he says. Uh, yeah. Only I know how much my twisted right ski knee still hurts.

"That was probably my last at bat. At least it was a home run."

Yes, indeedy, this is the kind of happiness in our world that just makes you sick. Close by those holey jeans beats the heart of a true survivor. Under those scabby knees is pluck. He's only forty-five and he has a hardy comeback shell, so we'll see.

"I'm too old to be running like that anymore," he muttered, making me very sad at his sadness and even more tender toward him than his raggedy jeans and scabs made me be. Where's the hydrogen peroxide for a boo-boo like this?

All I know is: I will never again be so happy cracking a crab leg.

Part 2

As it always does after every Dark and Stormy Night, the sun stumbled up the next day in the east, dragging our eyes open with it. This was our cue to drive to Idaho for our family reunion.

We were enjoying a wonderful ride. I was stretched out on a pillow on the way-back seat of our van, reading a wonderful book all by myself, while my four little darlings, in the middle seat and (oh bliss!) riding shotgun, stuffed themselves with green grapes and goldfish crackers without mom's interference or rationing.

Naturally then, Steve started to feel sick. He pulled the car to the shoulder at 11:30 a.m., too dizzy to drive anymore. He felt so sick that he wanted me to take him to a…gasp…doctor. Gasp even louder…a hospital…quickly. Wonderful.

Steve has a high tolerance for pain. If he were, say, wearing thick scabs on his left knee all summer long from ball games, he wouldn't flinch if I picked them off. Or if his finger was broken from catching a fastball, he'd rather set it himself than pay a doctor to do it. I know this because he's already done that. What he *can't* do is watch his wife get poked with an epidural during labor or prodded in her abs during an episode with an ovarian *smirk*. He *can't* watch our cute little babies get poked with immunizations. He has to look away or crumple.

So he was finally worried about himself. He and I whispered on the roadside while our children giggled and made blowfish window smears at us from inside the van. But moms can recognize Worried Blowfish. Steve wondered aloud, "Maybe my wounded leg is getting gangrenous and poisoning my whole body."

I'd never heard of such an outlandish condition, but it might be possible. Anything's possible. Right?

I jumped behind the wheel, speeding southeast toward Boise and a hospital, making siren sounds in my mind, while he stretched out as much as a tall man in pain in the back seat can do. He lay sideways in our Astro van, writhing occasionally, like a crab about to be boiled and placed alongside cocktail sauce and gourmet crackers. As I peered at him in the rearview mirror, my continuing tenderness toward him from the night before swelled up like too much cupcake batter in overfilled wrinkly paper baking cups. I was truly that tender, and not just because I was hungry. Oh, I could have stopped in LaGrande or Baker City, but my husband's sick-making softball wound seemed too exotic for Podunk towns. My tender feelings made me ambulate over the speed limit.

Then the sky cracked open. Wonderful. Here I was, acting all festive while I gripped the steering wheel with white knuckles, headlights on, flashing lights and siren in my mind, speeding too fast for conditions, at a pitch black two o' clock in the afternoon on a two-lane highway in the state where I grew up, never known for torrential downpours, squinting through a 100-year Idaho monsoon, praying it would not be so, but thinking my husband might be dying of Softball Gangrene.

To scare us a smidge more, Steve made me stop every fifteen minutes so he could crawl out to the side of the road to tinkle and winkle enormous, lengthy waterfalls into the borrow pit. He was a nectarine in a food storage dehydrator.

Even with all the snacks and fruit and drinks in their tummies, our kids and their baby bladders didn't writhe that much on this trip, nor did they need to winkle four times every hour. Insinuating into my tender feelings snuck a small whiff of comic relief...something to do with coyotes marking their territory. But I smothered the mocking thoughts when the rearview mirror revealed my children's big eyes and quiet mouths at their father's behavior and mommy's white knuckles. Baby panic.

"I think my kidneys are shutting down," he moaned from the back seat in a stage whisper. As things were getting more dramatic by the minute, a thought flickered through the way back of my mind. Not cute like Tinkerbell, but buzzy annoying like a mosquito. *If your kidneys are shutting down, why are you sending cloudbursts into Idaho borrow pits so often?*

Like how a summer breeze at a ballpark blows a mosquito or gnat or a little piece of Cracker Jack out of your child's ear, all the drama arising from my imagination swept that lone reasonable question aside. The siren sounds left my mind, as the next ridiculous question buzzed over and over: *When you're tired, why are the bugs stuck to your windshield as big as Godzilla?* Thanks to my training as a theater major, it's hard to stop at just one dramatic thought.

Thankfully, we careened into Boise at 4 p.m., following the blue hospital signs (One really appreciates blue hospital signs after one has reason to follow them.) until we found St. Alphonsis Hospital, right across the street from *The Idaho Statesman* office, where my niece worked.

With kids trailing behind us, I snatched a wheelchair from a little old Pink Lady and pushed Steve to the Emergency Room myself. While two non-medical types processed our paper work I called *The Idaho Statesman,* searching for support. Just give me another crutch. We'd have one for hope, one for encouragement. Two crutches are better than one at holding up the big fat slob called misery. Jenny ran right over, now also anxious. This was another reason I drove to Boise—to worry my niece.

By 5 p.m., the children had had enough of the novelty of an ER waiting room—the hacking coughs, the feverish eyes, the bloody farmer fingers fresh chewed by wild hay balers—so Jenny took them to her house.

I continued upright on my single crutch of hope. Steve continued his fifteen minute treks for bathroom monsoons. Nurse appeared in our room, took Steve's blood pressure, and asked about his symptoms. We described them in detail. Young Resident with a soft Southern drawl bustled in, we itemized the day's events in time-line precision again; he took notes on his clipboard.

The drama unfolded like this: From midnight to 6 a.m. Steve replayed the softball game in fitful semi-sleep, tossing, turning, and scrabbling. At 7 a.m. Steve nursed a 20-ounce Dr. Pepper to stay awake in the driver's seat. A practice we don't often do, since A: we don't often have such traumatic nights before a long drive to a family reunion, and B: we know that the tannic acid in caffeine is used to make our good leather baseball gloves.

At 8 a.m., the first rest stop, I filled up the empty Dr. Pepper bottle with water because he was still thirsty. He chugged that one down, and at our 9 a.m. rest stop, filled his bottle again and guzzled that one down. Over the course of two hours he had consumed 60 ounces of liquid. (I don't know about you, but I can winkle after four minutes and six ounces.) He felt dizzy right after the Dr. Pepper but waited on his borrow pit sessions until 10 a.m.

"Do you suppose the Dr. Pepper was tainted?" Steve wondered.

"Maybe. Anything's possible. Right?" I replied.

Resident couldn't keep it straight. He kept popping in and out of our room. Dizzy first or Dr. Pepper? Water and Dr. Pepper together in one hour? No wonder you had to pee. Water at the rest stop and then dizzy? Dizzy and then pee? Peed and got dizzy? Peed Dr. Pepper?

At 6 p.m., Nurse asked Steve if he could urinate so they could enjoy one last lab test. Darn if he didn't have more in there to comply.

At 7 p.m., feeling abandoned, I wandered into the hall to see if that was true. An EMT sauntered innocently toward me. I snared him as pitifully as I could, "Can you help me please?" I described how slow, how molassesey, how trapped we were in the Twilight Zone.

He laughed at me. "The average wait time in an emergency room is four hours."

We were agonized, then, as we should be. Just little mice in one of those sticky traps that seem so inviting but never, ever let them go. Typical, mediocre, sticky hairless mice, we accepted our fate. Not special at all, as both Nurse and Resident pretended we were. Since imminent death was draining away like...well, you know...and Steve was in slow but capable hands, I was antsy to read the wonderful book I had enjoyed so many hours ago. I read out loud to Steve to help him pass his sticky trap time.

Four chapters later, young Resident re-entered our world and asked us the exact same questions we had answered two hours ago. No wonder it's a four-hour event. We answered with the exact details, as before. Was this a trick? A pop quiz?

By now Steve felt a little better, cutting way back on his writhing, moaning, and trekking. Resident was "trying to get all the information straight to discuss it intelligently with the

ER doc." Could *we* not discuss it intelligently directly with doc? No wonder it's a four-hour event.

It was time for my own trek to find Wee Willy Winkie. One lone person, a new Nurse, passed me in the hushed hall near the women's bathroom. "Emergency is very busy tonight," she smiled. Sure, uh huh. I was so convinced.

At 9 p.m., Steve felt pretty darn good. He wasn't dizzy anymore. He didn't have to tinkle *or* winkle anymore for anyone. Our four hours were up. As if on cue in this drama, enter young Resident with Dr. ER himself. We presented our story for the last time in an encore presentation. Ta-dah!

Dr. ER diagnosed it like this: "You had a huge jolt from the caffeine in the Dr. Pepper. Sometimes when men stand up to urinate and they're full of caffeine they get really dizzy."

This Horrifying Condition has a special name and our doctor pronounced it slowly and described the gruesome details, but I have since forgotten it all. Wouldn't you? Anyway, it's not uncommon for a man to get this Horrifying Condition. It makes me glad of the inconvenience of sitting to eject my liquids.

"You had an overabundance of fluids," he continued. "We think you'll be fine. Your urinalysis shows nothing abnormal. Just don't drink anymore Dr. Pepper and pee standing up."

Sometimes you *can* have too much of a good thing and you *will* experience Horrifying Conditions because of it.

And the gangrenous leg?

Overly dramatic. Way, way over.

"Oh," says Dr. ER, "it's an age thing. Some people, not everyone, have a tiny muscle in their calves called the plantaris, which at odd times will just snap in two, and then atrophy away in the leg. It happened to you. I know how it feels because it happened to me."

His prescription: *warm up carefully, play sports carefully, be careful.*

Snap and atrophy. Nothing you can do. It's an age thing. An age thing! Welcome to the true Twilight Zone. Like an Alka-Seltzer tablet in a glass of water, like Dr. Pepper dregs in an open 20-ounce bottle—you fizz for awhile and then you're flat.

If there is anything more unattractive than this, kindly let me know.

At 9:30 p.m., Steve felt fine. Our four-plus hours in the ER were a prank on us. It was a miraculous self-cure with competent professionals attending. We didn't care that he'd wear a doughy lump in the back of his ankle for the next two years until his plantaris dissolved. We counted our blessings—he didn't catch Dunlap's Disease. We checked out feeling fine. They told us they'd bill us. Fine.

This is the kind of happiness that just makes you sick.

We had a fun sleepover at Jenny's house, even a great night's sleep on her floor. No tossing, turning, or scrabbling. My husband was going to live. My kids got to eat pizza and drink root beer for dinner. No caffeine allowed.

The bill from St. Alphonsis Hospital arrived in our mailbox four days after we got home from our fun family reunion. The charges were not nearly as bad as I thought they would be after The Terrible Horrible Tinkley Gangrenous Day. The bill was only $137.00.

In Washington it would have been $1,370.00

I'm glad I held it till Boise.

Big Humiliation
1973-to the present day

    It's funny how you can learn something really well and then flunk big tests.
    In 9th grade math we learned how to subtract larger numbers from smaller numbers. Magically, the end result is a "negative" number. I learned this strange truth and got A's on the homework. When we took the first test on these negative numbers, I panicked at my desk, staring at the equations like I had never seen the concept before. My mind was a total blank.
    When Mr. Taylor walked past my desk during the test, I looked up, incredulous, and whispered to him, "You can't subtract a larger number from a smaller number!"
    He smiled down at me in sympathy and said, "Sure you can." He must have been puzzled at an A student's metamorphosis. As I walked out of the classroom door after the test, I remembered everything about negative numbers. The veil of my memory bank suddenly jerked open again and I was mortified at my malfunction.
    The next day I held the test paper witness of my failure in my trembling, sweaty hand, then crumpled it up and threw it out. I'll never forget that red F.
    Four years later, in the spring of my senior year, rejoicing that all tests were over and we had passed everything in the world to pass, we partied.
    Word spread quickly following grad night. After commencement ceremonies ended, some of our friends and classmates went up to the mountains for a kegger, and got so drunk they couldn't drive back out. The next day, when they got hungry, they killed some farmer's poor sheep and roasted it over

an open fire. I never asked for the whole truth. "Don't ask, don't listen" is handy in preserving friendships.

My circle of friends, the non-substance-users, partied in Mike's grandma's backyard. Oh wild, you say. We danced and played night games like Sardines and knocked back root beer floats—way less sophisticated than puking on sagebrush and eating stolen mutton.

No drinking means never drunk. It's never been one of my big public humiliations. I do have lots of others, though.

I've tripped on invisible sidewalk cracks in front of observant boys and men; forgotten lines, dance steps, and song notes, morphing into a squawking, peg legged parrot at auditions; mingled among friends and strangers with spinach accessorizing my teeth; and tumbled down ski hills spilling off "yard sales" of sports gear directly under chairlifts full of applauding skiers. But most often, I've put my feet (and whole legs) in my mouth without ever desiring to be a contortionist.

In 1992, my brother died of AIDS. After he'd been gone from us for eighteen months, business moved us to Seattle, where he'd spent the last ten years of his life. We'd lived there about two years when, one day, I felt prompted to read the obituaries in the *Seattle Times*. I never read the obituaries. On that particular day, the life of my brother's partner was abridged in one small paragraph, synopsized in five sentences. I was crushed that I'd let so much time pass, tending to my own family's needs without tending more carefully to my friendship with someone who had mattered very much to my brother.

My husband and I drove to the wake at Chad's sister's home, where our fellow mourners quieted to a deafening hush when we entered the house. We were met with hostile, curious, accusing, and sympathetic stares. They must know how little time I spent with Chad. They must think I hadn't loved him or wasn't grateful to him for caring for my brother. My shoulder blades itched. I hugged both sisters and we murmured condolences back and forth, as sisters do.

I realized that Chad's family and friends were all tipsy on the way to becoming smashed. That little frame house tensed, carrying the weight of this odd party, following our movements, squeezing us all. The chatter grew louder and faster, time and motion slowed down, setting up house under the wooden beams, putting down roots where I didn't want them. Sometimes you're loneliest in crowds.

Steve and I acted our parts in this parlor drama, smiling, shaking hands, picking at the obligatory finger foods before inscribing loving words about Chad into the guest book. I meant them.

I respected all our grief and didn't want anything to sully it; but tiny paper plates, cheddar cheese, and paper cups exposed us. Each sip of Sprite was a delicate balance. Choking down my last gulp, I focused on the faded yellow linoleum of the kitchen floor. My brother, dead now for ten years, had ripped out a floor like this when he remodeled his old frame home in north Seattle. I needed a good cry in a long, hot bath.

You learn the same lessons over and over; and still, there are times when that thick veil just drops over your memory like it's never been pulled back at all. I turned to Charlotte, the tall, the drunk, the fierce, took her hand in mine and started to say *I know you're not religious...* But she cut me off in a drunken temper. I thought she was going to punch my lights out. What I had started to say was *I know you're not religious in a formal sort of way, but I'm so grateful for the prayers you offered for our brothers.*

She shrilled on and on about all the prayers she had said for her brother, for my brother, and that God had heard her prayers, not just mine. I listened, until she sputtered down and stood staring dully at me, swaying a bit on her heels. Steve and twenty spectators watched quietly. Cindy moved closer. We were a triangle of sisters. The vulnerable points between us kept us apart and held us together.

Mortified, I wanted to sink into Charlotte's floor, even as I struggled to make things right. Me drunk? No, but under the influence of an empty mind.

Life is not a party, it is a test.

Her tirade over, I began again, "I'm sorry. I certainly didn't mean to offend you. What I was trying to say was that I've been grateful for your prayers. I understand you're not religious in an organized church sort of way, but I *am* grateful for your prayers. Like you, I know God hears us. He answers all of our prayers, even if it's with a *no* instead of the *yes* that we want."

She sniffed and nodded and got it, but I don't know if she forgave me. I hugged both sisters again before we left. Hopefully, they won't remember much of that day.

I, however, will never forget that lonely F.

A stumble may prevent a fall.
                    -English proverb

Queen On A Hot Tin Roof
1972

    Big happy spectacles are so much fun.
    After a grueling rehearsal month and a thrilling pageant night, who do you think was crowned Blackfoot's Junior Miss? Well, guess again, smarty-pants. It was me.
    You might think that the Three Stooges were our judges, but no, somehow normal people plopped the crown on my Aqua-Netted head.
    This was a sweet little victory after many personal defeats; not a revenge…just a s-a-wweet. W*ill wonders never cease?* as my mother used to say. She didn't say it out loud to me on the starry night I was crowned, but I'm sure she said it to someone. That phrase would usually burst spontaneously out of her mouth like a root beer burp. For example, it filled the air at noon every third Saturday of the month when I managed to make my bed.
    Forget about the classic Miss America one-piece white Esther Williams swimsuit—dancing on stage in front of the whole world in a one-piece blue phys-ed suit is excruciating enough. You'll remember that those suits not only "flattered" every body type, they also revealed, through pit stains, how nervous you were about playing Dodge Ball. But phys-ed suits are the small price you pay if you want to win the Physical Fitness award in the Jr. Miss pageant.
    You can glide around your coffee table all you want with Vaseline on your teeth and *The Complete Works of Shakespeare* on your head, side-stepping your Jack Russell terrier as she tries to lick you with love, ("Out, out, damn Spot!") but unless you have nerves of steel magnolias on pageant night, you'll

never win a Poise and Appearance award.

To win the Judges' Interview Award, you must be able to think coherently on your seat, with ankles crossed primly, hands calm in your lap, and appear completely charming. Dimples help.

To snag the Academic Award, you want straight A's for four years. If there is a grade-point-average tie among the super-smart contestants, you must allow the judges access to your most private diary pages, going all the way back to your crush on the two Tommy's in second grade.

Winning the Talent Award requires you to practice something cultured and refined for 16 years. Anything will do, as long as you can fool all of the people some of the time, or perform in a pink tutu...or long flowy dress...or you should be Meryl Streep.

To win the Miss Congeniality Award, you must express sincere love to everyone, be totally nice all the time, and be able to tie everyone's prom gown bows equally perpendicular to their spines before they go onstage for the evening-gown competition. Congenials don't want their fellow competitors wearing lopsided bows.

My name was called twice for these individual awards. The silver charm for Physical Fitness sparkled in my hand as I thought: *My best friend standing here next to me just got out of the hospital from an emergency appendectomy two days ago.* So I give all the credit for that win to Cathy. And then the Poise and Appearance charm glinted up at me, too. I give all the credit for this win to Vaseline, Shakespeare, my dog, and a few years of private dance classes with Miss Barbara at Barbara's School of Dance.

You can go ahead and call it the Poison Appearance award, but as you laugh with derisive mocking it may indicate that you're just jealous, not really mean. And not really Congenial, either. That's OK. Here's an insider's secret: we contestants call it Poison Appearance. But as I cradled this second silver charm in my palm, I was thrilled and grateful to be Physically Fit with Poison Appearance, since all the competitors were dang fit and poised.

Congrats to Peggy and Cathy and LeeAnn for collecting the other silver charms.

After the six preliminary awards were given out, the big moment arrived. Peggy was crowned as second attendant and

Cathy was first attendant. The next insider's secret is that everyone else is now doing some mind pleading: *I just have to win or I might die.*

I had lost lots of things lots of times in front of my peers and knew well what that felt like. It stinks worse than a dead carp after six days in sunshine on the back seat of the family Buick. I felt overdue for some luck.

My friend Melanie sat next to my dad and mom in the audience and was eager with details when the whole shebang was over. She sneaked a peek at my parents as I took the queen walk down the runway holding red roses and "smiling amid tears of joy" as *The Blackfoot News* reported in next morning's newspaper. Mom was crying a bucketload; Dad had tears running down his cheeks, too. Melanie hugged me and told me she thought his tears were especially cool. I thought they were more than cool.

I'd never heard of such a thing about my dad. I'd never seen him cry—even when I was 13 years old and popped the tractor clutch too hard as he stood on the running board behind me. I spilled him forward into the fender because I didn't warn him I was driving stupid. It chipped the bone of his kneecap and he had to walk with a cane for three weeks after my little farming mishap.

Hearing that Dad cried on the night of a silly-serious show thrilled me as much as hearing that one last name called out at the end of our pageant spectacle.

OK, put your hankies away now and ask: *What were the duties of Blackfoot's Jr. Miss?* Cutting the ribbon for the new Ace Hardware Store in the Blackfoot Mall, visiting the Chamber of Commerce with four other BHS students to show off some school projects, and having lunch with the Kiwanis Club, the Soroptomist Club, or whoever—but not that many free lunches since Blackfoot is a small town.

These days, I hear that rather than receiving crowns, trophies, robes, and roses, Junior Misses just get boring old achievement certificates. What are you sponsors thinking?

The big diamond crown was part of my outfit at all town events. This naturally tempts one to feel superior to those without crowns.

There was always a little dichotomy, a conundrum, a silent argument, a heart condition going on in my sternum—shy about sticking out with sparkles on my head while poisedly chewing chicken-fried steak—OR—being perfectly OK with, and feeling too natural about, sticking out while cutting and chewing in small town clubs.

The shy side of this fame debate came from being my dad's daughter. The second side of the squabble arose from being a drama queen from the day I crawled out of the ooze of my diapers. My fellow townsfolk didn't sport crowns to the cattle auction, to A&W Drive-In, not even to the Potato Museum (*Free Taters to Out-of-Staters!*). So I could rest assured that my outfit was pretty much one-of-a-kind.

Beware adulation. It is dangerous.

At 16, heady with a glass tiara on my noggin, I told anyone who didn't live in Blackfoot that I was *Miss Blackfoot*, a distinctly different queen-type than *Blackfoot's Junior Miss*. The title *Miss Blackfoot* just rolled off your tongue quicker. But because Blackfoot has never had a *Miss Blackfoot*, I took creative license to label myself so, without the excruciating discomfort of parading around in a one-piece white Esther Williams suit in front of a distinguished panel of judges—usually consisting of the Pocatello Chamber of Commerce president, an Idaho Falls piano teacher, and the Rexburg school district superintendent.

(An aside here: As a judge from a competing city, wouldn't you be tempted to choose the homeliest, klutziest, most vaguely talented person on the stage? Hmmm...makes me pause. And perhaps that's why I've never been asked to be a judge.)

Whatever kind of queen you are, you know that parades are always the best choice for seeing a lot of action. You get to ride in a luxurious automobile and do the Beauty Queen Wave. *Elbow-elbow-wrist-wrist.* Repeated every second for five miles or two hours, whichever comes first. Do the math—that's 7,200 waves—if you do your duty with a heart full of song and much gusto.

Don't mistake this wave for the Rodeo Queen Wave, which goes: *Pointer finger+middle finger-shake fast-shake fast-shake fast*...from the wrist, with one hand, while holding the reins with the other, staying upright on your galloping horse, clinging tightly with both legs, one lap around the rodeo arena at Mach 3 speed without grabbing the saddle horn. Two very different waves. Talk about Poise and Appearance. *Pointer finger-middle finger-shake-shake-shake*...whoa! Now that's hard.

My queenly duties died off in the summer after school was out. Becoming tired and bored with the slave life of moving sprinkler pipes through hay fields with my older brother, Dean, and wanting a new adventure but being too shy to call the adult adviser person to our Jr. Miss court, even though I knew her well, and not wanting to seem a gloryhound, although I certainly was one, and being a seasoned drama queen, I took it upon myself to impersonate an adult chaperone pageant person for the benefit of all.

At this point, I feel that you're disillusioned with my reign.

The War Bonnet Round-up Parade was going to prance through Idaho Falls in August—yeehaw!—and my attendants and I just *had* to be in it. Shouldn't Blackfoot, *The Potato Capital of the World*, be represented with crowns and gowns in our neighboring city before their annual rodeo began? Spurs and horse pooh can take you only so far.

After reading *The Blackfoot News* article outlining all the juicy parade details, I pondered my options—1. No call, no parade, remain bored. 2. Call Mrs. Peterson, be a gloryhound, beg for a parade. 3. Impersonate an adult chaperone, call Idaho Falls, hear NO, maybe get arrested for impersonating an adult chaperone. 4. Be brave, impersonate an adult chaperone, call Idaho Falls, hear YES.

I had made a few prank phone calls in my day. I was a good little actress with three years of BHS drama classes under my belt. I was an optimist in those days. You can do this, Juls! With shaking fingers I dialed long distance to Idaho Falls, to the office of the parade organizer, Colleen Filmore.

"Hello?"

"Mrs. Filmore?" I asked in my lowest, most Meryl Streep exquisite, confident sounding adult chaperone accent.

"Yep, this is Colleen."

"Hi Colleen. I'm calling from Blackfoot. Hey, (*Hey?* Oh that was adult sounding!) the Blackfoot Junior Miss group is wondering if there would be a spot in your parade for them, and so I'm calling to check on the requirements of participating." I didn't give my name. Duh. Or Mrs. P's. It wasn't a lie!

"Oh, we'd love to have 'em in the parade! All I need to do is add 'em to our list here and give 'em a number for the line-up."

"Wonderful. Do we need to send you any bios or fill out an application form?" (Oh, how adult! What the heck do you do to get into a parade of this magnitude?)

"Nope. I've gotcha down. Please have yer girls be at the Westbank Hotel parking lot at 7:30 a.m. ready to go, y'know, dressed beautiful, all that good stuff. Our parade organizers'll be wearin' orange vests and carryin' clipboards. Jist check in with one of them."

"All right, thank you very much."

"Oh, one more thing."

Yikes! Don't ask me for my name and number! Is your refrigerator running? Slam.

"Jist be sure you bring yer own driver. We'll have a car for 'em from one of our auto dealership sponsors. Jist bring your own driver."

I let my breath out with a small pop. "OK, will do. Thanks again."

"You betcha. Thanks and we'll see yer girls in a couple weeks."

Click. Sigh. Shiver, shiver, cosmic shiver.

Another phone call, and Cathy and Peggy were all for it, blissfully unaware of the surreptitious finagling. We coordinated our prom formals—official queen attire and best of all for the city, free. We wouldn't clash. Cathy would borrow my red one, Peggy would be pretty in pink, and I would stay cool in white eyelet. We had our hair, makeup, and clothes planned before we ever had a driver.

I recruited Dean, home from college for the summer, assigning him several jobs—chaperone, navigator, translator between the orange-vested officials and our court, and most importantly, driver. The fact that he was collegiate leant our adventure a smidge of maturity.

To be honest, I can't remember if I called Mrs. P to fill her in, but if I did it went something like this: "Hey, guess what? They want us in the War Bonnet parade."

"Oh, that sounds fun for you girls! What do we need to do?"

"We just show up and bring a driver. Dean's agreed to do that for us. They'll provide a car."

"Wow, that's great, isn't it? I hope it's a Porsche, a convertible! Do you want me to come with you?"

"Only if you wanna come. We'd love to have you, but, ya know, Dean makes a good chaperone."

"Yes, he does. OK, then, I probably won't. I have a golf weekend planned with my husband on those days. Make us proud!"

What she didn't know never hurt her. (And may I say today: Hi, Mrs. P! Luv ya!)

Dean drove us up in the long green family Buick. Going north on I-15 through the Snake River Valley lava rock landscapes we sang along to Carly Simon's "You're So Vain," chewed red licorice, and wondered what color our dreamy sports car would be. We smoothed our skirts nervously and giggled a little too loudly. I couldn't stop doing either.

Dean's main motivation in going was the hope that he'd get to drive a red Porsche convertible. We made him agree that red would clash with our gowns, then we put our hopes on something just as exotic—the James Bond car, a black Porsche, or a white convertible of any type—a small dream for three innocent teens from Blackfoot, Idaho, and a kind big brother.

At 7:29 a.m. we finished great harmony with the Beatles. *"Yesterday, all my troubles seemed so far away, now I need a place to hide away..."* The green Buick turned a triumphal entrance into the Westbank Hotel, the most luxurious hotel in Idaho Falls...um, the only hotel. We had our gowns. We had our crowns. We had clean elbows and wrists. We had our driver putting on his Driver face as he stepped from the car. He put on his hat. He put on his dark aviator glasses. We found the starting point of the parade. We found the official orange-vested man. Never let them see you sweat the fact that you are without an official Blackfoot chaperone.

"Oh, right. Here you are, number 86 on my list... Blackfoot Junior Miss. I think your car is just over here."

We followed our orange-vested man, gliding past bands, floats, politicians, horses, and other queens, smiling, nodding. Royalty was all over the backs of everything convertible—yellow, silver, red, white, blue, their legs dangled down into back seats, poised. Royalty stood next to hard-top Porsches and Cadillacs and other exotics, poised to allow orange-vested guys to help them up onto step stools, thus on to sponsored luxury. Where was *our* sumptuousness?

Oh, no. I spy with my little eye...something in the distance that makes my blood run cold...*No, please, no. Oh, orange-vested man please say it ain't so. Oh, orange-vested man, I'm so disappointed in you.* He stopped right in front of it. The last naked car without a royal thing poised anywhere in sight.

"Yep. Here ya go. This is your car. Number 86. Have fun ladies and gentleman. Oh, yeah, there's a nice blanket inside that you can put on the hood so you don't get your dresses dirty. If you get up on the top, just don't fall off." I squinted at him to see if he was kidding. His poker face guffawed and with a cheery wave he strode off to make someone else's day. Not even a step stool.

No. But, yes, it *was*. What broke our hearts was what it *wasn't*. What smashed them to smithereens was what it *was*—a Chevy station wagon with those awful woody-paneled sides. Red. With woody panels. A station wagon. A red station wagon.

This is what happens when you are your own inexperienced agent. 86 me right now, won't you please. Just right now.

We stood shoulder to shoulder in a solemn line, contemplating our fate in silence. Dean finally looked at me, rolled his eyes and said, "Oh, sure, this is the James Bond car we were all dreaming about."

Sick in thick denial, we had to bend over with laughter. It was either do that or puke. Washing our carefully made-up faces clean with tears and snorts and snots, all slushy and mushy, we pondered our fates.

"O-o-o-h, d'you think they did this on purpose?" Peggy asked.

"It's 'cuz we're from Blackfoot," Cathy said.

"It's the revenge they've planned for three years. Ever since we crushed the Bonneville Bees 104-6 in football," I agreed, "After all, it was a national record."

"Well, shoot, 104 to 6. *Guinness Book of World Records*. Glad they didn't take it out on us," Dean said, sighing. "You want me to go get the Buick?"

Sighing back, I replied, "Heck no. Let's climb aboard this boat, this Big Red, and be queens!" The funk was over. Dean helped us clamber aboard. Ungraceful, we didn't even need a step stool. Procuring that item must have been the adult chaperone's job.

Just then the local, overly dramatic Channel 8 weatherman walked by, his tiny entourage following. I slid off our yacht. I'd written comedy skits starring this man, impersonating him many times. Wearing Dad's old gray suit, rubbing my fingers feverishly through turbulent chalk weather patterns I drew on the blackboard, stirring up storm clouds of chalk dust to wipe on my suit and hair, with copycat spit flying out the sides of my mouth from time to time, I had given my all to entertain the masses, just as this man had entertained us for years. He *loved* weather. He *was* weather. Everyone loved this loud, lisping, leaned forward, full-lipped, wavy-haired passionista. I loved him. He was TV royalty. I asked him for his autograph. He gave it to me with laughter and a little spit, and posed with us for a Kodak moment.

He didn't ask for my autograph. Lloyd Lindsay Young never knew how many laughs I had gotten as him.

After that I could have died a happy paradester without the parade. Almost.

Little kids loved us and waved back. Adults just stared. Come on, adults, why can't you wave back? What is wrong with acknowledging the cheery spectacle as it passes by? Have you lost your wave ability? Take a lesson from the happy children, people. Life is much more joyful.

Looking for reciprocity to our friendliness, we waved all the way down to the curbs, because that's where the children sat. The children and the elderly possess common sense and the shining qualities of fun and friendliness. We were forced against our wills to ignore all humans between the ages of 12 and 66 because they snubbed us first. Can it get more juvenile than that? If we had been wearing spurs and horse pooh, we might have fared better.

Since our royal court had been in drill team together, thus in many parades together, we knew about parade pacing. Your basic parade doesn't just flow along without hiccups. It's art that imitates life. And like the freeway at rush hour, there's always some rubbernecker causing a backup. Can't we all just flow along? What we didn't know was that stopping often with your dance troupe on foot is not the same as stopping often with your bums on the hood of a big old Chevrolet. Rub-a-dub-dub, six buns on a tub...

Our buns began to sizzle after the first half-mile, although it didn't happen all at once. Like that frog in the lukewarm pot, we were happy for awhile without realizing we were being cooked. Curiously, I felt a stinging sensation but couldn't quite put my finger on it. My fingers were busy waving. Maybe it was just seat bite from sitting on a hard surface for fifteen minutes on my broken scar-tissued tailbone.

So, we smiled and waved at the gutters while, without knowing it, our buns burned up. It dawned on the three of us simultaneously.

"Is your bum sore?"
"Hey, is this hood getting hot?"
"Are your buns burning?"
"Did you know the car was going to get this hot?"
"I didn't know it would get this hot."
"No one told me it would get this hot."

We were 16-year-old queens, not 56-year-old car mechanics.

We squirmed from cheek to cheek trying to find a cool spot. It became a game—one potato, two potato, three potato, four! Five potato, six potato, seven potato, more! No cool spots. Zip. Nada. None.

Some fun parade. To our dismay, we morphed into Rodeo Queens. Hang on with one cheek, cool the other, *elbow-elbow-wrist-wrist, shake, shake, shake...* faster than we intended, faster than Poison Appearance would have us behave. Whoa! Don't get bucked off Big Red! We slithered about like cats on a hot tin saddle. Don't get bucked off into the gutters below or you'll have to stay behind with icky old non-waving adults. Don't get bucked off 'cuz then you'll have to run to catch up in your heels and your long dress and your diamond tiara and they'll see you sweat and you'll never be able to clamber back aboard Big Wild Woody Red because we don't have a stepstool and no one's going to get off to give you a boost even if we are all good friends. The heat made us delirious.

Dean realized what was happening only after I turned around and grimaced against the windshield, my hot breath steaming up the glass, mouthing, not screaming, the words so our public wouldn't be disillusioned, "OUR BUMS ARE ON FIRE!"

During the next parade pause so some angry clown could scoop up horse poop, Dean put the car in park and stepped out. "What d'you wanna do?"

"Help us climb up on the roof," we whimpered.

"Okay." He tried to pull, boost, and cajole each of us up as we hastily, daintily lifted our skirts, (ah, cool 90 degree summer air) desperate to scale the windshield and scramble onto the roof. It was too slippery. We just couldn't make it in our long skirts. Where's the Physical Fitness when you need it most? Where's the Poise and Appearance when you need it best?

The Blackfoot beauties slid back down to H-E-Double-Toothpicks.

"Wait, I know. Here's the blanket from the back seat." Dean folded the white thermal blanket, arranging it under our behinds. It was as thick as a lunch napkin from A&W.

Ah, a reprieve! The parade moved on. The blanket helped for exactly three minutes before it, too, wanted to go up in flames. We slid as far up the hood as we possibly could, half sitting on the windshield, letting the soles of our feet burn up for awhile. We slid back down. Up we went, down we went, up down, up down. Dean peeked out through our hips, maintaining his dignity as Driver, the only one who maintained any dignity at all.

And so we cowboyed up at our first War Bonnet Round-up.

As we *elbow-elbow-wrist-wristed* our adoring crowd of gutter children and skittered around the hood of Big Red, we were just one big happy spectacle.

Making a big spectacle of yourself is the punishment for being your own chaperone. Making a big spectacle of yourself is the punishment for deliberately choosing to be part of a spectacle.

Even a satin gown, a sparkly crown, and elbows and wrists in place can*not* a big spectacle prevent.

Come on...wave back at me please. *You* are not the big spectacle when you wave back. That's the job of queens who only *wish* they were angry clowns. Wave! I know you can do it! Come on and wave, people!

You might help save some hot, *cross* buns.

The future belongs to those who believe in the beauty of their dreams.
                    -Eleanor Roosevelt

One Cute Boy and One Fast Dance
1970 onward

It's murder loving a teenage boy—slow death that you relish every moment of. Every minute is torture as you wait for stuff that either comes too fast or never seems to arrive.

*   *   *

He stood out among all the other kids at our youth conference. He would be the perfect hero of a romance novel, even though he had no bulging biceps. Even though, or maybe because, he could chirp like a cricket on a hot summer night and could mimic Kermit the Frog perfectly. Miss Piggy should be so lucky. Come to think of it, I guess she is.

I knew a few things about him and was sure I would like to know more. I knew that he was a senior, just about to graduate and go off to college; he was a member of our youth council who planned events like this one for other lucky teens; he was nice and polite and fun to be around. He had a great sense of humor, and as he moved among the crowd, he joked and laughed and made everyone feel like a friend. He was someone my mother would have loved for me to bring home. Unfortunately, they never met.

Six feet tall and graceful as athletes are, I wondered how far he could hit a baseball, how long it would take him to pin LaVerl Horrocks, the champion wrestler from my high school. I wondered how many consecutive free throws he could make or if he had the hands to catch our quarterback's pass from halfway down the field.

His dance moves set my feet and head in motion involuntarily, like some stupid hip-hop marionette. He's good, I mused, studying him closely. I caught a Mona Lisa smile playing on my lips and smothered it with my right hand. I wasn't about to point anyone else to my hero, My Boy. Everyone will have to guess who I want to dance with tonight, I thought. I'm not giving myself away to this bunch of gomers. That would be way too embarrassing.

The oldies rock band Time Piece cranked it up and let it go and the lead singer put his heart and soul into "Louie, Louie." We screamed with joy and mumbled along to words we will never know. These tubby, middle-age rockers had my crowd of teens in the hip pockets of their Wrangler jeans.

The semi-decorated gym was not too dark to see who was with whom, or too lit up to make you self-conscious about your moves. Red, white, and blue balloons taped around the walls shimmied to their own beat with the flurry from the dancers and the open doors welcoming in the night breeze. A rainbow of balloons arched over the stage, framing the aging Time Piece. Already the younger, hyperactive, non-dancing fourteen-year-old boys reached for the stray balloons at the end of the stairs, untying them furtively to avoid the Big Chaperone Eyes. Sucking out the helium, they sang along with the band, a squigee version of their squigee little selves.

This inspired other little geeks across the room, the fringe-hangers, not brave enough to dance, not honest enough to leave the gym and go to bed early. Removing one balloon at a time from the walls, they answered the wild calls from their beast buddies near the stage. Like young bucks trying to figure out what to do when a doe passes by, they bugled in helium voice or popped a balloon at the backs of the plain, less-secure girls who moved in small herds or danced together as a pack. These sneaky bullies only pretended to avoid the chaperones.

My hero, My Boy, was mature. No mugging balloons. You could tell he'd popped a few balloons years ago, but now he knew how to ask a girl to dance and then made sure she had a good time. He interacted. He entertained. He made wishes come true.

When the kids opened up the circle in the middle of the floor, daring dancers rocked through, demonstrating their specialties. My Boy took his turn, doing a hip boogey move with his feet, arms in perfect rhythm, smile balanced. He looked fine.

The crowd was generous and clapped for everyone, even the balloon-popping doofus whose only claim to fame was an incredible double-jointed upper torso that made us all go "Eeewwww."

My Boy chose the cutest, liveliest girls to dance with; those with dignity and twinkling eyes and the kinds of smiles that draw boys in to see what all the zest was about. I have hard work cut out for me tonight, I thought, as the band blasted out "I Wanna Hold Your Hand" and the hard-driving beat kept teens nailed to the floor, bodies gyrating, lips syncing.

The tall, dark Handsome Guy sitting next to me on the table by the door struck up a conversation between songs and I screamed back at him, trying to be heard. In a sudden switch of mood, during "It Don't Mean A Thing If It Ain't Got That Swing" when the trumpet player was trying to be Duke Ellington, we laughed at the little adolescent man down on the floor in front of us being schooled in complicated steps by the blonde girl who obviously had had swing lessons.

Handsome Guy and I had some great dances together and when "Boot Scootin' Boogie" leaped out at us in the dark, we both gamely tried to learn the steps. It took me half the song to get into line-dance heaven, but Handsome Guy was six-feet-four in his stocking feet, lukewarm for country, and not so big on line-dancing. He lagged. We laughed. We tripped. We still had fun.

I danced with one eye on My Boy and one eye on my own fun. Two eyes when I was with Handsome Guy. But when was I gonna have a chance to dance with My Boy?

Every time he looked my way I shifted my gaze. The last thing I wanted was for him to notice me watching him. That would kill our fragile social flower before it even had a chance to bud. I had to keep my senses hot and play this thing very cool.

When intermission came, everybody crammed around the serving table for cookies and root beer. I noticed that My Boy picked up two drinks, giving one to Cutey Pie, who had been hanging around him all night. That's class. Cutey Pie made goo-goo eyes at him until the cookies went stale. They joked together as a group gathered, and then all of them clowned around doing Pee Wee Herman impressions, and I could tell he was having a good time at this simple party. The old band guys finally filled their big bellies with water, root beer, and chocolate chip cookies and then got back to work.

I glanced over at My Boy and caught his eye. He smiled from the deepest depths of his blue-green-as-the-ocean eyes, lifting his head in acknowledgment of my smile. Success! His smile was genuine, charming, and infectious and I grinned big right back at him without smothering it.

My hopes rose like a helium balloon safe from geeky hands. Without one steady girlfriend to monopolize his time maybe he'd find his way over here closer to me. Of course, nothing was stopping me from going right on over there and inviting him to dance, but somehow I knew that just wouldn't be cool with him. He was the one who would have to ask me. But darn if he wasn't taking his own sweet time about it.

After all, my cuteness factor matched the cuteness factor of the girls he was dancing with. Didn't it? It's death to look too eager, too needy, too smiley. I rediscovered that truth tonight when I asked two of the little geeksters to dance. They turned me down! Maybe they were embarrassed to be seen dancing with an "older woman" or even dancing at all, or maybe they saw my offer for what it was—a mercy invitation. They need to learn to dance at some point in their little cretin lives. Still, it deflates your ego when the geeksters turn you down.

I sneaked a peek at My Boy again while the band was crooning the Commodores' "Sail On" and he had his arms wrapped around Artsy Girl in the black beret, who had kept surveillance on him all night. He looked up again and straight into my eyes. Another big smile. He knows how to work this room.

Finally, My Boy said goodnight to this chick and started over to my table by the door. Handsome Guy, who had stuck by me all night, sat shoulder to shoulder with me, our legs dangling down from the table, swinging together to the beat. My Boy kept coming, not intimidated by Handsome Guy. Maybe he'd noticed that H.G. was secure enough to encourage me to dance with other guys. My Boy stopped in front of me and slid onto the table beside me. My heart skipped a beat.

"So, you havin' fun?" he asked.

"Yeah, are you?" I shined my most beguiling smile at him and didn't mind Handsome Guy's keen interest in the two of us.

"Yeah, this band is pretty good. Everybody's dancing."

"So," I just could not stop myself. I could not resist. "When are we going to dance?"

The band started up again with "What I Like About You," the music rolling smooth and fast past our table and out the doors, into the starry, starry night. Crisp air poured back in, and the dancers stayed cool in the hot pursuit of mysterious pleasure and dreams come true.

"Right now," he said and stood up, holding out his elbow for me to take.

A perfect, charming invitation. I placed my right arm into the crook of his left arm and we literally skipped out onto the floor, the center of attention at our position right under the noses of Time Piece. I had been waiting for this kind of fun all night.

We grinned at each other as we started a pattern so in sync it surprised both of us. We jumped and jived and made a big motion of our dance. The other kids stood back and watched and clapped, some dancing on the fringes around us, until they all joined in.

Oh, it was smooth, all right. This way and that, symbiotically moving to new steps and old, and every one was pure joy because I could tell he was having just as good a time as I was. He answered my laughter with his own. He looked me in the eyes and there was the reply I needed to see.

We danced so big and fine I was afraid I was going to swoon. Now, the ultimate in embarrassment would be to lose all energy, to stumble and fall here, or faint dead away. Or even sweat like a pig and pits myself in front of the whole crowd and this one Deluxe Boy. Pacing, pacing, pretty mama.

The song stopped way too soon. Our finale ended with hands clasped and feet whirling in a pop-square-dance move. We both stopped dead in our tracks on the last cry of the final note, and, still looking eye to eye, we clapped and laughed. The crowd clapped and cheered.

Then suddenly, in the middle of all this noisy commotion, my intuition was sharp in a stillness I hadn't felt all night.

Overwhelmed, my heart skipped a beat and my throat constricted. How silly. I didn't trust myself to speak to him. It was all over way too soon. You think the best times will go on and on forever, but they never do. You pray, you hope, you will them to, but they never last. I sensed the moment with My Boy was gone. At least it was a lovely memory to last forever. A "best time" that I could replay whenever I wanted or needed to.

We hugged. A big, rocking, bear hug.

"That was so much fun. Thanks for dancing with me, Mark," I smiled, trying to catch my breath inconspicuously.

"Hey, you're a good dancer. It was fun. Thanks for the dance, Mom," he replied.

My Boy moved away toward Artsy Girl as I walked slowly back to my table at the door to the beat of "How Do You Mend A Broken Heart?" Back to my own tall, dark Handsome Guy of twenty-eight years. My baby boy, my last child at home, was preparing to leave the nest. Off to college in the fall of 2002. This was a milestone. After years of hanging out with teens, my husband and I would never again chaperone a youth conference with any of our own four children in attendance.

"Well, did dancing with your son make your night, or what?" My Handsome Guy hugged me.

I nodded, still not trusting myself to speak.

Yes, it's murder loving a teenage boy. A slow death that you relish every moment of. Every minute is torture, living through changes that never seem to arrive, but that, in reality, come in a blink.

Just one fast dance with one cute boy. It was all I got.

But it was enough and more.

Retro

On summer's porch,
stair-sitting
by light of full moon,
bare legs are
sixteen again;
denying their marathon
of a million miles
through this lifetime.

Stretch them slowly out, down,
over two steps
to concrete.
They glow
flawless and strong,
blushing under kind, old orb.

Stay still
until midnight,
when Luna glides away,
dancing behind treetops.

-JJO
1997

We can't give our children the future, strive though we may to make it secure. But we can give them the present.
                              -Kathleen Norris

If you don't believe in God, besides being an atheist, you will be very lonely, because your parents can't go everywhere with you, like to camp, but God can. It is good to know He's around you when you're scared, in the dark or when you can't swim and you get thrown into real deep water by big kids. But...you shouldn't just always think of what God can do for you...
                              -Danny Dutton, 8, from his 3rd
                              grade assignment to "explain God"

The List of Places I've Waited
1993

What is one of the most likeable smells on earth? That's right...industrial paint. Take a long whiff and kill a few thousand brain cells. Why do they make it smell so fine?

Today we're painting the old commercial oven for our new bakery and I kill a few cells I can't afford to lose. The 16-year-olds who do this for kicks on a regular basis, the ones we see on nighttime TV with fried-egg brains, have whiffed too much stuff.

Steve is such a neat painter compared with me. I'll happily slop paint on the floors, the walls, my pants and my hair before I'm through. I cook the same way.

Cooking is as dangerous as painting. Scientific studies show, for example, that roasting marshmallows over an open gas flame on the stovetop in your apartment is dangerous to your health. Flaming goo on the pointy end of a red-hot metal clothes-hanger is all fun and games until someone loses an eye.

We'll get cancer from roasting marshmallows. Scientists will make sure we do. The flames, the smell, the taste, the sticky...all comfort. The crusty black charcoal sides from impatient roasting...instant cancer. And s'mores? Armageddon.

With visions of puffy-caramel-fluff dancing in my brain, I finish painting my half of the oven and sit on the edge of the oven racks—an uncomfortable spot—but a handy place to watch Steve. After seventeen years of marriage I still like watching him. Must be love with a capital L. Oven racks are a close spot for waiting and for conversation with my best friend.

Some waiting can be productive enough to yield interesting rewards, like a perfectly toasted marshmallow, a daydream, a grocery list, staring off into space to rest your brain, forgiving, forgetting, talking with friends, family, or yourself.

Some waiting is not productive at all, just stinkin' torturous. One day I may come down with some strange infirmity and the doc will say *Ah, yes, Mrs. Oliver, this disease stems from the odd places and times you've waited for your husband. But there is hope and good news. The cure is a life of decadent luxury with maid service, gourmet chef, bon-bons, good books, back rubs, and sunny beaches.*

The real cure is that my husband waits for me like I wait for him, wherever those conditions find us.

I've had time to be in my head, pondering this tall man I live with—praising him, observing quirks, remembering forgettings, angry with him, loving, liking, admiring, insulting him, laughing silently at him or out loud with him.

I have worked out much of a long, great marriage waiting in unusual places for my best friend.

In a stupor of reverie, not at all helpful in finishing our pressing practical painting task, I fall silent, contemplating some of the weird places I have sat waiting for my man. I share them with you, knowing you will be tender—as my bottom is becoming on the oven racks. Tender like a perfectly roasted marshmallow.

- 8 airplane rides
- Hot summer sidewalks: 3460 North, University Avenue, and Center Street
- 1 tall tree stump in Pasadena before the Rose Bowl Parade
- 3 wooden bridges
- 2 wooden planks crossing two different rivers
- 11 living room floors

- 25 different ski hills at 5 different ski resorts: Sundance, Alta, Park City, Snowbird, Whistler
- Swimming pools in Utah, Hawaii, Arizona, Washington, Florida, and California
- 9 different truck stops in Idaho, Utah, Oregon, Washington, and California
- 2 rocking chairs
- 6 river banks
- 9 lake banks
- Beach towels on beaches
- Behind 1 bush on a deer hunt
- 1 tent on a deer hunt
- Lawns of green grass: ours, friends, relatives, schools, public parks
- Empty beehives in fields, towns, and backyards in Utah and California
- 1 fat tree stump in the Sierra Mountains
- 1 tree limb—waiting for a camera to auto-snap our engagement photo
- Under 6 quilts
- Picnic tables: wooden. plastic, aluminum

- Couches: comfortable and uncomfortable
- A plethora of blankets on: beds, lawns, river banks, 1 pickup truck bed, and 1 car
- 1 peach box in a peach orchard
- 1 apple box in an almond orchard
- 1 fishing tackle box (about as comfortable as oven racks)
- 3 airport lobbies: Los Angeles, Salt Lake City, Seattle
- Towels: beach and bath
- *The* Waldorf-Astoria Hotel
- Porch stairs in: Lewiston, Provo, Blackfoot, Hamilton, Yellowstone Park, Sun Valley, Kaysville, Salt Lake City, Issaquah, Bellevue, Fall City, and the San Dimas of *Bill and Ted's Excellent Adventure*
- Beds: twin, double, queen, king, hotel, motel, ours, friends', family's and 2 hospitals
- Truck beds: Chevy, Nissan, two-ton, diesel
- 3 toilets
- 1 dance studio floor

- Car seats: Honda, Buick, Oldsmobile, Nissan, Chevrolet
- Countless doctor lobby chairs as the injured or the sick
- Countless doctor lobby chairs as escort to the injured or the sick
- 1 cement bench
- 2 bike seats
- 5 hospital chairs (different than doctor lobby chairs)
- 1 silver garbage can
- 1 wooden fence rail
- 4 bathroom floors
- 7 curbs in the Western United States
- 1 red canoe
- 1 Laser two-person sailboat
- 2 bakery tables
- Our favorite folding beach chairs (which never saw a real beach in their entire lifetimes) at: 30 T-ball games, 380+ little league games, 4 river banks, 3 lakesides, 2 swimming pools, 2 grade

school play grounds, 6 junior high cross country meets

- Bleachers at 40+ basketball games in junior highs for school and city leagues, 30+ high school basketball games, 80+ high school baseball games, 12 high school swim meets, 8 high school track meets, 16 dance recitals
- Bleachers at 4 high school graduations, 2 college graduations, with more to go
- Theatre seats for 10 junior high orchestra concerts, 9 play rehearsals, 8 dance rehearsals
- 2 folding chairs at: 1 high school graduation and 1 college convocation
- On my feet in: sandals, flip-flops, high heels, sneakers, slippers, ski boots, moon boots, cowboy boots, bare feet
- Innumerable church benches and folding chairs for church meetings
- Big league baseball stadium chairs at: 2 major league ball parks for 10 major league games, and 1 high school graduation

- 2 passenger train dining cars
- 1 big pillow: with choking belly laughter, waiting for him to turn the page to read aloud more romantic poetry in his best Scottish accent
- 1 bale of hay
- 2 bales of straw
- 28 campfires
- 1 treehouse
- 1 commercial oven rack, cool not hot

Being stuck in places – like tree trunks, beach chairs, and oven racks—offers two choices:
1. To wait and ponder and work things out…or…
2. To wait and ponder and whack someone in the head before you run screaming in the opposite direction.

Everyone should practice marshmallow waiting. The results will be so warm and delicious you'll want to gobble them up in one bite. But savor every morsel. Then…

Have s'more.

Where have *you* waited for *your* best friend? Make your own list.

```
Such as we are made of, such we be.
                            -Shakespeare
```

Bad Hair Day
1967-2007

I am a streaker.

You know you've overdone it when you walk into your high school admin office to get lunch money from your mom, the secretary, and the principal's jaw drops to the floor and he can't stop staring as he shouts at your hair, "What have you done to yourself?"

As to my streaking, I confess...I should have kept the lid on.

It's really hard to pull long hair through the teensy holes in those plastic frosting caps. And the eensy-weensy crochet hooks that come with the caps? You can't knit Barbie a string bikini with those things.

In 1971 I had a good idea—if you can get a *few* subtle streaks in two hours with an eensy crochet hook through teensy holes, then you can get *lots* of subtle streaks in a couple minutes without the hook, cap and bleeding scalp.

So, yep, why not throw away the cap and hook and simply *paint* the frosting on with your fingers? That way you don't poke divots in your skull and you won't crochet your long hair into fishnet stockings fit for a long-legged sailor and his long-legged wife. (Remember the sailor family? *Have you ever, ever, ever in your long-legged life seen a long-legged sailor with his long-legged wife? No, I've never, ever, ever in my long-legged life seen a long-legged sailor with his long-legged wife.*) Have you ever, ever, ever in your long-haired life seen a long-haired high-schooler with subtle highlights?

I should have kept the lid on.

Today, we cringe at shelling out $150 to a professional stylist for highlights, plus another $50 for a haircut to go with that color. Why, that's 200 Arby's on a 5 for $5 deal! My hairdresser is excellent (I *do* love you! I do, I do, I do!) and she does like to eat and pay rent, but there are no highlights worth that much money. Am I the only person disgusted with the professional ransoms on our heads?

So, every two years, I forget my troubled past.

Let's blame it on math. By investing in a set of $35 clippers and cutting my husband's hair, my three sons' hair, and trimming my daughter's hair, over 27 years I saved our family a bucketload of money. As an untrained civilian stylist you can create a pretty good hairdo if you concentrate, though losing focus will cause you to swerve off the hairline path and you'll cause an occasional *oops*. Like a doctor, you learn to say *there* instead of *oooohI'msosorry*. Now, let's set the price of these family haircuts at a conservative $10 a pop, pretending that everyone goes to a cheap cuts place or a beauty-school student. Home-cutting my family's hair has saved us an estimated $16,200! Now *that's* a story problem worth solving. And we didn't even include home perms.

If we estimate family haircuts at today's prices…well, it's a number so shockingly high it boggles the mind. It's an über-google or something. Only in the past two years have I sent my husband out to strangers to get his hair cut. I'm busy with projects and he chooses to get shaggy right as deadlines hit.

We've both chosen not to let him do my hair. So, forgetting my youthful troubles, I trotted over to the drugstore and paid $20 for the *expensive* box of color. *I had vowed silently to myself, and out loud to my husband after the last do-it-yourself horror show months ago that I will never do it again… we can afford a few streaks now and then from a real stylist… I am too old to keep doing this…if my hubby can't help me with streaking I'd help myself…at a real beauty salon.* Even after these solemn vows in italics, the temptation of quick and cheap do-it-yourself gray coverage became too great to bear.

How many times must we learn the same lesson?

I bought the easy, two-step box for all-over color. It included an extra highlights sauce packet. The model's hair on the box looked closest to my all-over hair color with highlights, minus some gray roots coming in. I ripped it open with grim fascination, read instructions, unscrewed lids, followed everything to the letter, and—turned light pomegranate with tangerine highlights, which could be exciting under certain circumstances. Just not mine. I only wanted to cover a few gray hairs and escape the über-google price of my regular hair salon. Instead, I became an exotic fruit salad.

    I dialed the toll-free freak-out number on the easy, two-step box and was assured by the beauty operator that:

    A) I would receive a coupon for a new easy, two-step box of color.

    B) Medium Brown #5 would cover the red-orange of pomegranate/tangerine.

    C) I should wait 48 hours between colorings.

    D) I could beg my professional stylist to fix it but the easy, two-step company wouldn't pay for the fix.

    I enlisted Steve to pick up the $20 box of Medium Brown #5 on his way home from work. Pomegranate with tangerine should not leave the house—ever. I applied #5 the next day and my hair became...cherry cola. The beauty operator may have

    A) Lied.

    B) Been ignorant.

    Cherry cola is less red-orange than pomegranate/tangerine and a slice more normal in its own way, but not *natural* like professionally applied light brown with dark blonde highlights, which, no matter how bad your style is, allows you to leave the house unafraid each and every day.

    Cherry-cola hair is movie hair. I think Meryl Streep won an Oscar for her cherry cola hair in one of her best movies. I bet she used special shampoo. And in *South Pacific* when the girls sing "I'm gonna wash that man right outta my hair" they must have used special tropical shampoo. Coconuts and cherry-cola. I only have regular shampoo and special dog shampoo, which I didn't try. I was not thinking. If special shampoos can win awards, or rid a girl of men and fleas...hmmm, maybe next time. (*Next time*? Who said that?)

    Being a streaker also ruins good bath towels. Even when you think you've gotten all the bad sauce off your head, there's always some hiding in your ears. We use retired beach towels to dry off our dogs before they come inside on rainy days, but I never remember to use the dog towels to dry my newly colored hair. After I've lost my mind, it's asking too much to remember the mud room and its assortment of dog towels. So, buh-bye, master bath ambience, you now have tangerine on your deep cocoa.

It all adds up: Let's do the math one last time. Two $20 boxes of color, plus six hours of frenzied (Wasn't there a Hitchcock movie called *Frenzy* on this exact topic?) mixing, applying, rinsing, conditioning, rinsing, drying, panicking, grieving, plus déjà vu all over again to cover your surprise fruit salad, plus one new bath towel to replace its predecessor. It all totals up to about $420. As this mathematical calculation has just proved, my professional stylist is cheap at twice the price! With tip.

I kept the cherry cola on my head, styled it; and went through my week as living research for this very essay. It was a scientific experiment. Here is a partial list of comments I received from people who know my "before" and "after":

Husband: "Oooohhh, there's a redhead in my bed." (Don't you just love him?)

Close Friend: "Whoa! (She's a horsewoman.) Did I miss something? (We laugh together.) Was this to give Steve a new experience?" (I explain only some of the research.)

Daughter: Silence

Granddaughters: "Did you know how to braid your hair?" "How can you know how to braid your hair?" (Less of my cherry cola flying free to shock them. I braided their two tiny all-natural blonde heads of hair and we all had fun.)

Male Adult Friends: Silence, with some sidelong glances (One held his tongue with supreme effort.)

Fairly Close Female Adult Friends: "I didn't recognize you! I love your hair!" "I like your hair!" "Your hair just keeps getting longer and longer."

Other Female Adult Friends: Silence, with some sidelong glances

Teenage Female Friends: "I love your hair!" "I love to dye my hair!"

12-year-old Boy Cousin: "Did you dye your hair?" (Count on 12-year-old boys to always be honest.)

14-year-old Boy Cousin: Raised eyebrows (On hearing the conversation with 12-year-old boy cousin and my explanation that this is a science experiment.)

Other Adult Female Friend: "I wanted to tell you yesterday that I think your hair is just gorgeous! Look how I try and cover my gray. I'll have to call and get your secrets." (She has beautiful, natural-looking, consistent blonde hair that you would never know is hiding a gray hair, PLUS, she does it herself, I need *her* secrets.)

   Much Older Female Friend: "Is that a wig?"

   Talented Regular Stylist: "Julie? I thought...Is that you? Wow! I didn't think we did your hair that dark!" (She gives me a sidelong glance, raised eyebrows, and a tiny disapproving stare; they wouldn't be professionals if they didn't.)

   Yes, I went back to the salon. I turned myself in and paid the bounty on my head.

   Talented Regular Stylist's Shop Owner: "She used a *box* color?" (With reeking disapproval.)

   Talented Regular Stylist: "Yes, she used a *box* color." (Too nice to reek.)

   Shop Owner: "Oh... yeah...I've never actually seen that particular color growing out of anyone's head before."

   I explained the scientific research, how it turned into a social science experiment, and then I said, "It's too dark for me. The color's not bad, I love the shine of dark hair, but it's too dark, well, and too red." (Oh, don't be silly.)

   Talented Regular Stylist: "Dark hair reflects the shine, lighter hair doesn't. It's fun to have dark, shiny hair. Yes, it's a bit too dark, but we can fix it! The highlights will cover most of the red."

   I filed this "dark, shiny hair" comment away in my brain box under "styling tips at home" just in case I want to pull it out two years from now. But let's all put a sticky note on that sticky note. It should say: *Please learn from past mistakes. Don't be a streaker. Just keep your lid on.* But if you can't, don't, or won't, just remember this: Most people will not notice your cherry-cola head. They're too busy being insecure about themselves to even notice you. This always makes for a good hair day. Or a bad one...depending on your needs.

   Wouldn't it be wonderful to be able to rescue a person's character as easily as it is to rescue their bad hair?

   Shop Owner left her own client, sidled closer to me, no longer disguising her sidelong glance, raised her eyebrows in my general direction, and gave a disapproving once-over, feigning admiration for my homemade coiffure. Her true opinion was unsuccessfully hidden from my scientific awareness. I returned her gaze in the big mirror in front of my chair. She wouldn't meet my eyes. She was busy giving me her *natural*, professional stare. This look is not meant to be hidden. It is meant to school you.

As was my shocked principal's yelp at my hair of so long ago.

I'm a slow learner.

What would life be if we had no courage to attempt anything?

-Vincent Van Gogh

I'm Just A Little Black Rain Cloud
2005

    Woke up with a rare headache. Is it due to the night sweat I just enjoyed or is it Black Cohosh? Sounds like a rock band. Hey, everybody—put your hands together for Black Cohosh! Welcome lead singer Medicinal Herb and his No. 1 hit—*Drench Your Sheets Eighteen Times Tonight*! Oh, yeah, he's singing my tune. I'm just one big slurpy mess all night long now.
    Maybe it's a dull boredom headache. Wonder what my friends are doing today. Don't have enough energy to want to find out.
    I need to call Tonia; need to check in with Michelle and Tricia; need to forget myself and go help someone else. I need to help my son pack for his next trip; need to obliterate all these pallid white walls with paint; need to paint the landscapes inside my brain onto a dozen canvases. I need to rewrite a query letter and finish a manuscript. I need to *not* get caught up in reading the library books spilling across my nightstand; need to file the papers spread out in a mess on my bedroom floor; need to...need to...need to...
    Want to just stay in bed and be quiet, alone with my books and my thoughts and my happy memories. Want to ground myself for a month. Old regrets pop up, like rabbits about to devour Dad's hayfields. They stare at me with big sad eyes. Sing it loud, Black Cohosh!
    Drag my journal notebook out to write my morning pages, to get the pus out of my brain, to get on with better writing. Children and husband, family, friends, strangers, pets, me, the world—all are in morning pages. No one should take it personal. It's just unworthy gunk. Let it go. From brain to

fingers to pen. Today it doesn't take me one and a half pages to reach truth. I get there in the first paragraph.

My hand scrawls so fast I don't recognize my handwriting, as the hurts my child threw at me resurface. Today, for once, I don't blame myself for this child's choices, but the stings linger.

For breakfast in bed, a Pink Lady apple. I'm roused by this small crisp taste, its juicy swirl of color. Pink Lady knows herself and buoys me with her certainty. She gives me hope and energy enough, on this rain-cloud of a day. An apple a day...keeps what away?

Don't want to exercise, even though it's crucial to keep training pace for the marathon. Instead of running down the road away from my achy head and achy spirit, I surprise the dogs with sprints up and down the forest hill that is our front yard. It's steep, covered with downed maple branches, ferns springing back to life, and small gray boulders. I trot as fast as Dinah will let me without getting tangled in her tall Airedale legs. She grins big white teeth at me and thanks me with her loud Wookiee barks, her Chewbacca voice, leaping around my knees for joy at this unexpected playtime. Lucy, our little white Jack Russell shadow, tries to sneak a lick on my shins, her best way of giving love. Don't want it today.

Steve's clover seeds push up tiny heads of green, weaving a carpet on the path cluttered with dogs and rocks. It only takes three round-trips to exhaustion. Dinah and Lucy pant with me, their tongues dripping beads of sweat into the moss on the big maple trunk across our trail. Stair-stepping up and down on the fallen maple, I remember the fun of these repetitions with our four little kids, training all of our thighs for ski season in Utah. On those snowy hills we giggled, cried, screamed, and loved. My energy balloon suddenly deflates.

The silence of this tree is exhausting.

On the way back to the house, I pull a few weeds from between our Bird Nest spruces; haul the red shovel up from the slash pile at the bottom of the hill, where Steve left it; scoop up four piles of dog poop, mumbling aloud some dim-witted whiny comment about keeping tools in good working order and out of the rain. This extra spurt of activity burns out, snuffed like a sparkler on the Fourth of July. I'm faced with going back inside.

One piece of whole-wheat toast with butter and honey; one glass of vanilla soy milk. Then I wander around, wondering where to go next.

K.C. wakes, watches ESPN, and waits for a friend to pick him up to go golfing. Last night after Buddy's invitation, K.C. brought his clubs in from the garage, cleaning each one with a soft old T-shirt rag dipped in lemon juice. Buddy hasn't called back this morning, so after dialing twice and waiting two hours, K.C. drives away alone. Two nights ago, Buddy failed to call K.C. after promising the Sonics playoff game on his big screen TV; K.C. watched it here with us.

Buddy, are you still deep into bad habits and neglect, into your chosen addictions, trying to chase demons away? Buddy, did you not learn this lesson in high school? How many times do you want to learn the same lesson?

In this quiet house I climb the stairs to my art studio, ambivalent, bring down an unfinished oil painting, leaning it against the kitchen wall, where I can evaluate it whenever I pass by. My ineptitudes make me step back to scrutinize each baby step like I've never seen it before. It's impossible to achieve a stranger's objectivity. Visitors to an art gallery, pondering works hung under beautiful lighting, absorb strength and story through quick impact right in front of their faces.

I can only finish each piece of art after slow progress marked in stages, like marking the growth of a child. Comparisons are inevitable. What is it now? Where did it begin? What is it supposed to be? What happened along the way to divert its truth? It surprises me how often my art takes on a life of its own and wanders off in another direction.

For the first time in a week I can see precisely. Having my weaknesses appear so obvious excites me. There are some glaring odd spots in this sunset landscape. The color between the sky, the field, and the trees is false and there are too many bright spots competing for the focal point.

I'm such a beginner. I collect impact so slowly.

I love my sky, but feel silly, thinking it is magnificent, and knowing it's not. As I stare at it, I hear my beloved Idaho meadowlarks sing out one last quaver as night falls in this canvas, the backyard of my childhood, calling me long-distance from forty years ago. *Beloved* is a melodramatic adjective for meadowlarks, but it fits them. I adore these birds and miss them. Last week, looking at this unfinished landscape, my husband said, "I've seen that sky." He has seen it in my Idaho.

This painting started out as a bright sunlit bank of day clouds, shimmering into sunset. The more I've fiddled with it, I see now, the darker it has become. Less light, more night; less what it started out to be, more of the wildly unplanned. It's not happy spontaneous. It has become false. I've been overlooking the false that I painted in. I've been overworking the false. I'm surprised. It's taken on a life of its own that I need to point in the right direction.

Pleased with the adjustments of today, but knowing it's still not finished tires me out again. I try to cheer up with the motto "joy in the journey," but today this maxim is maxed out. My moods are *chiaroscuro,* light and dark playing off each other side by side, like the sun and cloud contrast in this painting. Sighing, I wipe the gel medium off my hands, pick up my brush, and wonder when the toxicity of an artist's environment will catch up with me.

Never finished, never satisfied. No wonder van Gogh cut off his ear.

For lunch some baby bell peppers, two red, two yellow and one orange, eight sugar snap peas, and seventeen baby carrots. Premature baby carrots. Who ripped them out of the womb so early? The tiniest carrots in the world, smaller than my new grandson's pinky fingers. I have no appetite, no desire to eat, not even chocolate. These things are easiest to grab. Lunch is an accident. Nutrition just came along for the ride.

I give in to library books. Outside to sit in the sun on one blue canvas camp chair, my feet propped up in the other, I hide my empty lunch plate underneath. Dinah sneaks in, greedily grabbing the pepper tops and licking the dish. "Get away," I grump at her.

Eight essays later, I wander inside with the dog-licked plate, pile on a few stale tortilla chips, slap on some drying, three-week old slices of Tillamook sharp cheddar, and nuke myself a boring pile of nachos. Hit the minute-plus button on the microwave. Stare glassy-eyed at the cheese bubbling on my second course without seeing it, and realize, too late, that minute-plus is too long. The cheese is over-zapped, transformed into crispy orange honeycomb flats on dry chips. Salsa doesn't save it. I shuffle back outside to eat without bothering to taste.

Eight essays more and I know I have to drag out my laptop and write about this stupid day of dull heart and brain pus. Is this what a hormonal day feels like? I haven't had a menstrual period for six months. My friends seem too young and far away to ask. My mother died twenty years ago, so I do not have her to ask. My father died six years ago; my brother, thirteen. There is so much gone out of my life.

I feel it today. I've been an *orphan* for so long.

Stare off into the forest, sit on the sunny porch for thirty minutes more, and know what I want, finally, after the wanderings of this day. I see it precisely right there in front of my face. Slow impact.

I'm waiting for Dad to surprise my brothers and me with a trip to Pete 'n A's; in 1965 it was his favorite hamburger joint on the road into town just over the old Blackfoot bridge. Mom will murmur that she has green beans to pick and put up and would surely like our help. Persuading no one, she'll mutter a faint protest about a pound of ground-round just sitting in the fridge, as she gathers up pillows and blankets enough for the six of us; doesn't even bother with the oatmeal cookies in the Tupperware on the kitchen counter. She likes her popcorn covered with butter-flavored ooze and lots of salt just like the rest of us.

After burgers and fries served in little lattice-cradles of red plastic, we're off to the Motor-Vu Drive-in to watch *How the West Was Won*.

We'll see if we can win it one more time.

I'm waiting. Mom, I'm bored and I don't have anything fun to do. Mom, I'm bored and I have too much to do.

I'm waiting. Dad, come gallop a horse with me. Come see how the eyes of the barn kittens are opening. See how mine are opening.

Today, my inability to heal this homesickness is a thundercloud hiding a bright horizon.

When you lean back in stillness and take a long, silent appraisal of the story on your canvas, you can't leave anything there you know is false. You can't walk away and call it finished.

No matter how much you fiddle with it, no matter how much you overlook it or overwork it, false remains false. False always comes with a price, because the laws of art and the laws of life have consequences. Perhaps someday I'll paint a masterpiece, just a little story of slow impact.

There is no drive-in in my forest.

I pick up the book, plow into the next essay to avoid going back inside to busy myself with some other pressing task, then stop and place it facedown on my thigh.

I sit in stillness, listening. Sheba, the golden retriever at my neighbor's house down the road, barks at her children to come and play.

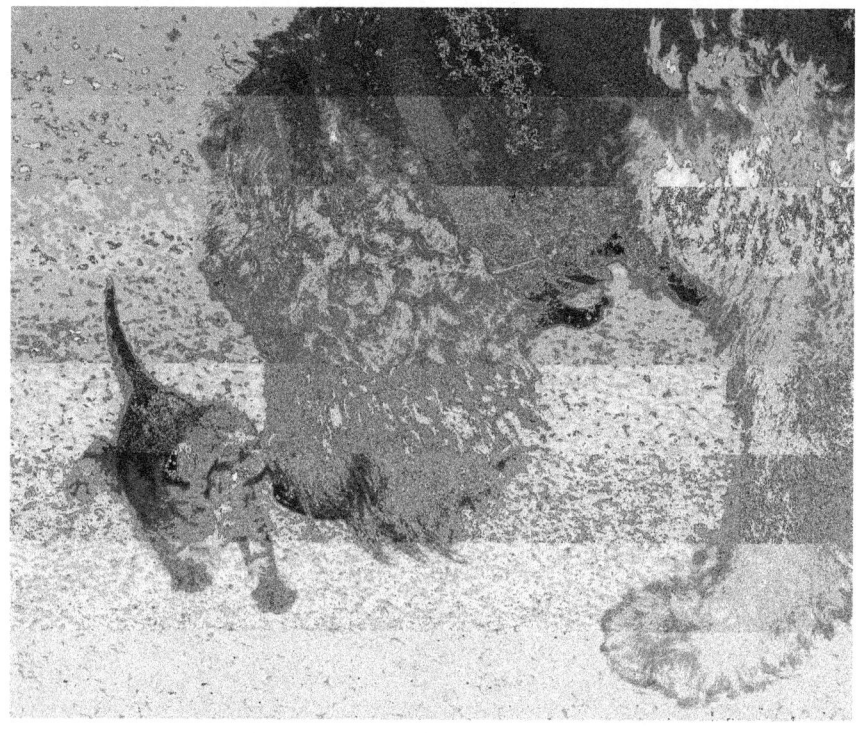

When you lose your parents in your 40s, it's a bad thing...
Even at 50, you just might think you're grown up, but you're not.
-Dovie Thomason

Yummy, Yummy, Yummy, I Got Gum In My Tummy
1991

"Does your chewing gum lose its flavor on the bedpost overnight?"

Trust me, there is more...la la la la...there is a whole lot more to this tiny tune and you repeat it over and over again several times. I'd share it with you, but I can't remember it right now. I'd never heard this little ditty until I met Steve and he serenaded me one night when he got tired of reading the romance poems of Robert and Elizabeth Browning to me in his best Scottish accent and my giggles slowed down. Ah, romance.

The more you know, the more you know you have a whole lot more to know. This new classic in my musical repertoire has elevated my status as an ignoramus.

On the autumn evening when I first cooked German Cabbage Soup with the harvest of cabbage and potatoes from my garden, lots of salt and pepper, and polska kielbasa sliced in savory rounds, a neighbor boy came sniffing through my kitchen, trailing behind my youngest son, Mark, on their way to play "Slide Down The Basement Stairs On Your Plastic Sled." If you pad your backside with a pillow before you plunk it down on the sliver of blue plastic, it's a fun game for the whole family, even with no snow it sight. Lots of giggling happens, and bruising. But it's worth it.

Mark was used to my scientific experiments in the kitchen, but 9-year-old Danny stopped short at the smell and peered over my arm into the shallow cooking pot, checking out our dinner grub.

"Ooooohhhh, you're making pig slop!" he exclaimed, insulting me without a second thought.

"Excuse me?" I wondered briefly if he'd like to try a big, fat knuckle sandwich instead of the slop in my pot, but I bit my tongue and let him continue.

"Pig Slop. I love Pig Slop. When my mom makes it she puts carrots in, too."

"Aaahhh...OK...this is called German Cabbage Soup."

"Nah, it's Pig Slop. Yum."

"Want to stay for dinner?"

"Sure!"

Cookin' mamas can't be sissies.

Even Steve's and my hardy German ancestry hadn't inspired me to cook this particular dish until my garden went wild with cabbage. I got desperate. Then I got lucky with this new old dish—a culinary success. Pig Slop *is* yum.

Garden desperation is the mother of gastronomic invention.

Take my zucchini for example. Please, take my zucchini. One monstrous out-of-control harvest for novice gardeners is enough to teach you that planting three zucchini seeds is plenty. Never plant the whole packet! Three zucchini seeds can feed your neighborhood, your community food bank, and the state high school debate competition. That is, if you can get the kids to eat it without tricking them. There is debate on that.

You can pick your friends and you can pick your nose, you can even pick your battles. But you can't pick your kids' battles and you can't pick your kids' friends and you don't want to pick your kids' friends' zucchini. Even if it ends up bottled and preserved in deep disguise.

Behind the closed doors up and down my street this year it was fashionable to bottle zucchini with a few fascinating additives. We were disguising zucchini to become pineapple. *This* is what a desperate housewife is all about.

This secret potion—a strange alchemy that could transform the lowest of vegetables into an exotic fruit—almost worked. What a fantastical makeover! If you closed your eyes and pictured the sand, the surf, the hibiscus of Hawaii, you could not tell the difference. You were there in your beachside *hale* with the cabana boys chopping fresh coconuts and slicing thick, juicy slabs of succulent sunshine dripping with juice. You were not in your white brick rambler with the grade school behind your chain link fence and sixth-grade boys throwing dirt clods at your cat.

Shut my mouth over heavily sweetened syrup and call me Pygmalion, but that was a canning season to remember! Oh, the joy cottage cheese felt alongside our fake pineapple!

We grieved when the County Extension Agents put the kibosh on it. Our paradise was brought back down to earth. Thank heavens. Something about not enough fruity acid and too much food poisoning. Well, there's a spoilsport in every town. A huge controversy ensued over private obedience to public servants. There was rebellion. There were certain homes you did not enter at dinnertime. This was not a smiley time in our neighborhood.

As you sweat and mature into a savvy master gardener, you learn not to plant zucchini at all. Lori, two blocks over, planted three seeds last year under my tutelage and in September shared her harvest with the entire school district.

"How'd you fit those into your garden?" she quizzed, puzzled when I delivered some gorgeous carving pumpkins in mock-thanks for her knock-and-run on my doorstep. I smiled dimly, still trying to figure out what to do with the fresh green canoe she had foisted on me earlier that morning. That's it! A canoe! My little Boy Scouts could carve out her zucchini and then we could float down the Provo River in our family-size love boat.

My part-German heritage includes aunts, uncles, and cousins who are gourmet cooks. We just concluded a successful, even fun, family reunion where some of our effort was directed toward compiling a family cookbook. It is well-loved by all, even without Pig Slop. (Zucchini was banned from the book.)

When my college roommate Jeri and I contracted Sophomore Spread because we ate big bowls of ice cream every night as freshmen—we told each other that it was a healthy snack—we devised our own diet to lose the Spread before the end of our second semester. We did this after being forced to sew our own jeans in bigger sizes than we wanted to publicly shop for. We'd also spent too much money on ice cream to buy cool jeans ready-made off the rack; so we oiled up her Sears sewing machine and revved up my old Singer.

As a curiosity item for my posterity, I saved a pair of these college jeans. The backside seam is ripped open. They've been waiting a long time to be repaired. Ever since that wild night in California on Jeri's and my first trip there—the night we polished off the "Pig Trough" at Farrell's Ice Cream Parlor in Santa Monica on our way to Disneyland—they've been languishing in a dark corner of my closet. Little did we know we could finish 44 gallons of ice cream at one sitting. Soon we rolled from jeans into caftans.

That trip to the valley to clean an ice cream trough became a major life goal once the waitress at Marie Callender's told us on All-You-Can-Eat-Soup-And-Salad-Night that Jeri could eat more soup, salad, and cornbread than the BYU football center could. I've always been so proud of her. Prouder than a zucchini-cum-pineapple.

I diverge from eating to sewing here. Excuse me, but it's all related. When you can take the lowest of vegetables, give it a makeover, and help it become an exotic fruit, you know you're on the road to Paradise. Those County Extension agents don't have a hold on us like our sewing machines do.

OK, let's get sewing. A special pattern follows, dredged up from the depths of my yellowed college files.

But before I give you our caftan pattern, I must not answer the call of the Rocky Road from my freezer. If I do, my hips are cooked. Pig slop.

On second thought, it makes me so happy to recycle these old jeans today (I'm going to Mod Podge these puppies and turn them into a grow box for next year's squash.) that I'm skipping the healthy snack. I'll just take the Wrigley's spearmint out of my mouth to plug both ears and then sing out loudly "Does your chewing gum lose its flavor on the bedpost overnight? La la la la..."

**Jeri and Julie's Funtime Caftan Pattern
For Lounging About and Looking Chic**
1974

1. Measure yourself from the floor, where your feet are, to your neck, where your head sits. You may need help getting this measurement down. Especially if you only have a metal ruler, a yard stick, or a builder's tape measure, which don't bend very well. It's easier if you have a seamstress's measuring tape, since it is bendier and can go over your curves better. You also can hold it down with your big toe if there is no one there to help you. But don't panic, because the nice ladies at the fabric store can get this measurement for you. They wear their special measuring tapes around their necks. It's best not to try to figure out how to get your cleavage to show. That would make this pattern too complicated and not modest. But this is the really important part: DON'T FORGET TO MEASURE ON DOWN BEHIND YOU, BECAUSE IF YOU DON'T, YOUR BACKSIDE WILL BE HANGING OUT IN THE BREEZE LIKE YOU'VE SEWN YOURSELF ONE OF THOSE COOL HOSPITAL GOWNS.
2. Write this measurement down so you don't forget it and then put that scrap of paper right into your purse so you don't lose it. Now here's what's so cool about this pattern: you don't have to measure around your bosom, your

waist, or "the widest part of your hips" as many patterns demand that you do! You don't ever have to know those numbers! Isn't that a happy thought? Funtime! Find a fabric store near you. If you don't sew, don't be afraid, because the women in fabric stores are usually very nice. Except for everyone in Fiona's House of Fabric, where they are surprisingly snooty. Maybe it's the name...Fiona...it's pretty French.

3. When you get to the store, or maybe before, if you have a calculator at home, take the inches you wrote down on the scrap of your phone bill and translate them into yards and inches. Remember: 36 inches to a yard of fabric, and your extra inches translate into fractions of fabric yards. Now still don't panic! The nice ladies at the store can do this intricate calculation for you.

4. Let's pretend you are 5'6" tall and your at-home measurement from both sides of you was a total of 124 inches. Remember: YOU'VE ADDED A SECOND HELPING OF BACK INCHES TO YOUR FRONT INCHES SO YOU'RE NOT HANGING ALL OUT IN THE BACK.

5. You can figure in a hem if you want to go to all that bother, or not, if you'd rather not. If you don't plan on hemming anything, be sure to pick out a fabric that will not ravel, or...SEE #4 AND #1 above for the flapping in the breeze reminder, because the flapping will come from all directions.

6. Pick out a charming bolt of fabric. If you don't sew, let me tell you that a bunch of fabric wound up tight around its cardboard thingy is called a "bolt." The same word as "running away rapidly from something in terror" and "what a crazy horse will want to do with you if you're not a horsewoman." But don't be scared...you're not in those situations.

7. Tip #6 is harder than it sounds, as there are scads of bolts in fabric stores and you'll find that you love many of them. If your budget

allows you can buy many pieces of fabric for many caftans. Of course, if you had that much money, more than a starving college student has, you could go to Nordstrom or Walmart and pick out one already made. But every woman knows that buying off the rack is less chic than having handmade couture.

8. Carry your bolt to the cutting table, where a smiley store woman will cut it for you. Don't you try to do it yourself. There are special methods at fabric stores for cutting material. Just stand there and watch—you'll see what I mean. These women are pros.

9. Now for the math. Show this nice smiley woman your scrap of phone bill. Before she cuts your fabric, she'll remind you to take that envelope home and pay your bill. She may or may not be able to do the math in her head, depending on her experience at the cutting table. Voila! (Excuse my French, I wasn't being snooty.) You will see that your inches from home—124—magically become 3.44444... and that number can just go on forever with remainders, but the smiley lady will put a stop to that and round it up or down and call it 3.4. In sewing speak that translates into 3 and 2/5 yards. Did you ever guess in your wildest imagination that your body needs that many yards of fabric? Now, here's the magic of the nice lady. On her cutting table is a special sewing yardstick screwed down tight to the table so customers won't want to take it home to make lots of mathematical fabric things. She will know exactly how much to cut for you. Don't worry about the width of your fabric. Most fabric is 45" wide and that should be plenty to go all around your widest points without you actually knowing what those wide numbers might be. Funtime! If it doesn't stretch all around your widest points, this project won't be that much fun.

10. Smile while she cuts your fabric. You'll notice that she measures twice and cuts once. Otherwise, she gets in trouble from the not-so-smiley store manager and has to take the messed up yardage home herself to make her husband some red and yellow tulip p.j.'s, or a caftan, depending on how much ice cream he's been eating.
11. Say "Yes!" when she asks you if you need any thread. She can point out where that is. Get some to match your fabric or, if you feel very daring, some contrasting color. The *chicer* the better.
12. Take your fabric and your thread to the front counter and pay for it. Put your phone bill in your purse. Go home. You've worked hard today. Have a snack: maybe some Neapolitan. Or maybe not.
13. Once you get home, lay your fabric out on your floor. You may want to vacuum up any stray dog or cat hairs first. Double your fabric over on itself (remember #1 and #4) because you want a front AND back to this outfit. Now go find your sharpest scissors. You might find them by the toaster if your roommate is done defrosting the freezer with them.
14. Here's the hardest part, but don't despair because you're almost done sewing your new outfit! Let me be clear: *cutting your head opening is the hardest part*. You can measure around the widest part of your head if you want, or you can just cut free-form, which I would not recommend because I've done it and I never did wear that free-form caftan. I used it to cover the tomato plants in my garden when the last big late spring frost attacked us.
15. Major alert! *Remember: Cutting off your head is the hardest part.* Follow these directions precisely: on the folded end of your doubled-over fabric you have to find the middle. Right in the middle of it. Use your yardstick to find the middle and either keep a pin there or your

eyeball. Take your sharp scissors and cut out a small semicircle (which is the same as a half but sounds more "sewy") on the fold around that middle you just found. In sewing speak: when the semicircle is held up and unfolded—because the fold is the diameter of the circle, not the circumference, sorry this is such a mathematical pattern!—it comes out as a whole circle, not two halves of a semicircle. I'm sure you can see this in your mind. (Mr. Taylor, my freshman high school math teacher would be so proud of this part.) Picture yourself cutting out a Valentine heart only without the pointy end and the two humpy tops. It's clear to me. Of course, I'm an expert at this, since Jeri and I developed this pattern ourselves as young college students and we both are 4-H'ers from way back. Make the semicircle small. (This next step is like cutting your bangs, so be alert.) You can always cut it bigger to fit over your head, but you can't shrink it smaller unless you purchased wool. In which case, you can wash your messed up caftan in hot water and throw it in the dryer, but then you'll have a caftan that will only be a dickie around a little yapping dog.

16. OK, pick up your almost-done caftan and drape that hole over your head, putting your new creation on your body. Stick your head out. Do you see? I'm getting so excited for you! Do you see that you've made a caftan? Funtime! Is it fitting? I hope so. If not, lay it down the way it was folded before and carve out a little more of that semi-circle. Pick it up and put that hole over your head. It's kind of like trying on a fresh Spudnut donut from Kesler's Market, isn't it? Only not quite that exciting. If your circle is crooked-ish, get some zig-zaggy craft scissors and pretend you wanted a French-type decorative edge all along.

17. Wait, you say, we've forgotten something! Yes, I know exactly what you're going to say. There

are things flapping in the breeze, but not from behind, as you have remembered to buy and double and cut so that your behind is covered. It is your SIDES that the east wind is blowing through, isn't it? Aha! You thought we forgot about your sides. This is where your thread comes in.

18. You must now figure out how to sew up the sides and I'm sorry to be leaving that all up to you. Don't come to my house about it, as I have one old Singer and three projects taking turns and gathering dust on my dining room table. So, you have three options: 1) If you don't have a sewing machine of your own, you can do it by hand like the pioneers did. 2) You can take it to your neighbor and beg her to do it. She might even hem the hem and neck for you if she's nice and smiley. 3) Lastly but not leastly, find your stapler and whack! whack! whack! Your seams are closed and you're all done! If you do it this jiffy way, be careful how you lounge about.

19. Lounge about! With joy, knowing you are a Renaissance woman in your own handmade creation that was Jeri and Julie's pleasure to design for you. Funtime!

Wow. Sharing that pattern took up more energy that I thought it would. I have digressed from my original food writing intentions. But since I still want you to have our special diet that enabled us to give up our caftans once and for all, I'm going to digress back to...

"Wait!" You're screaming at me. I can hear you from here. You don't have to be quite that loud. "Wait," you say softer, "I just barely got my caftan made! And now you want me to pack it in mothballs because it's going to be too big for me?"

That's a fair complaint. Trust me when I remind you that it's nice not to have to wear a caftan if you don't want to. Jeri and I mysteriously found ourselves in Sophomore Spread. It snuck up on us without our noticing it; once we realized this, we grew bored of our chic caftans and impatient with their amplitude. Even in a doubled-over, closed-up caftan, your backside gets really chilly when you're walking up the snowy hill to English 201 in January. Weight gain treats us so coldly.

After our dreaded realization hit and we decided to do something about it because we were tired of frostbitten buns, we developed our one short-lived diet—*The Bouillon Diet*. We trust that you won't recreate our original diet for yourself and then go off to your secret room and write a best-selling diet book based on our invention. Here's how it went:

Jeri and Julie's 1975 Bouillon Diet

1. Eat only bouillon at every meal. Crunch dry cubes or granules, or dissolve them in a cup of hot water, it's up to you.
2. While you eat your one bouillon cube at every meal, open your favorite cookbook and stare at pictures of real tempting gourmet food and pretend that this is what you're actually eating.

There. Isn't that easy? I could type this diet plan and publish it as *The New American Bouillon Diet* and it would become a best-seller in two weeks and everyone would lose weight for two days and clamor to give testimonials and I would make $55 billion off of you, but I like you better than that. And I'm sure you like other people better than that, too.

But honestly, don't bother following this free diet plan that I just gave you. Don't hope it will work. It didn't work. You will starve.

After eating too much bouillon (this takes two days) while wearing our chic caftans, we came up with this next diet, which really worked. It really, really works!* This is the best, simplest, cheapest diet you will ever try. I know this is so because it removed my Sophomore Spread. You'll never have to buy another book, tape, special food, bolt of fabric for a bigger caftan, or anything else diet related. I share it with you for free because I can just picture how darling you look in your new caftan.

Jeri and Julie's
Cabbage-Liver-And-Water Diet

1. Eat lots of cabbage, fried liver and onions, and drink lots of water.
2. You can eat other stuff, whatever you want, but only in small portions the size of one palm. Your palm—not the balloon-size palm of Oliver Oyl from the Macy's Thanksgiving Day Parade.
3. You can ONLY HAVE SECONDS of cabbage, liver and onions, and water.
4. In fact, you can have as much cabbage, liver and onions, and water as you want. Pig out on it if you want. Don't count calories!
5. Exercise.
6. Exercise some more.
7. Remember: You can disguise zucchini to look like Pineapple, but on the inside it's still a vegetable—the stuff that's good for you.

What, you say? You're clamoring for more of my recipes, patterns, and diets like the quality ones...wait, that's not you I hear...it's the Cherry Garcia singing my name from the freezer.

Quick! Protect yourselves, everyone! Sing it loud, sing it strong—

"Does your chewing gum lose its flavor on the bedpost overnight?

If your mother says don't chew it, do you swallow it in spite?

Can you catch it on your tonsils and heave it left and right?

Does your chewing gum lose its flavor on the bedpost overnight?"

Repeat several times. (Between bites of cabbage.)

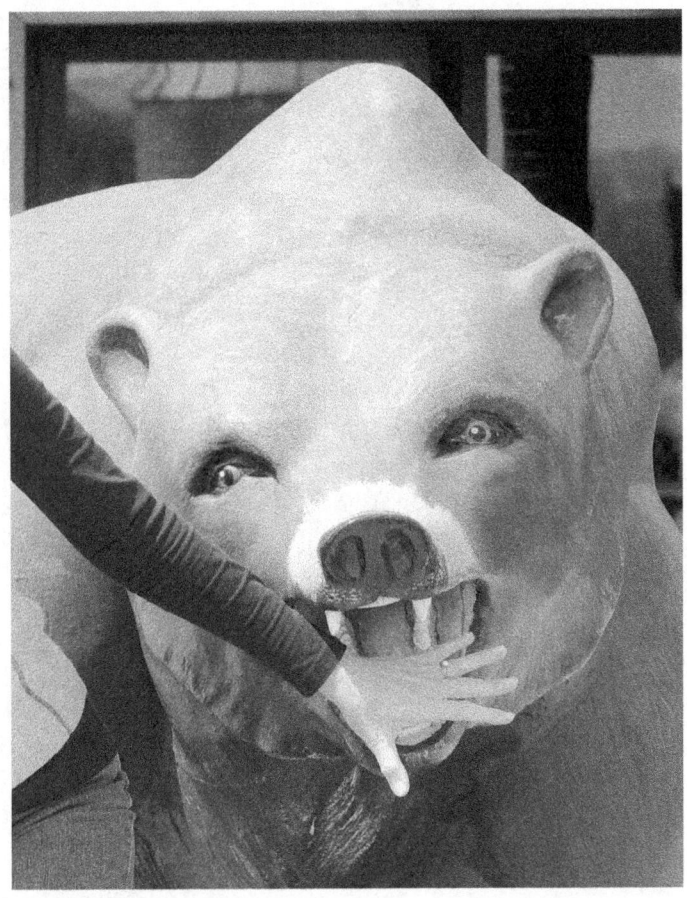

* You know I have to include a health disclaimer here for the folks who are way too trusting. So, consult with your family doctor before you try the Cabbage-Liver-And-Water Diet. Better yet, don't eat much of this diet. Jeri and I won't be responsible for anything bad that happens to you or your loved ones because of it. Nor will we sew you a bigger caftan.

The noblest of all dogs is the hot dog; it feeds the hand that bites it.

-Laurence J. Peter

Running Away To The North Bend Motel
1995

Love/hate relationships are everywhere under the sun.

Today Dr. Nixon looked at my hated spots. They're not tattoos or weird acne, they're basal cell carcinomas. I knew it intuitively, before he carved into my flesh in the most extreme skin exfoliation I've ever had, and sent tiny parts of me off to his lab for close examination. Love the sun, hate the damage.

Today I looked at my daughter in seething disgust, as if she were a basal cell carcinoma needing to be scraped off me. And she looked back at me out of the corner of squinty dangerous eyes, as if I am her hated spot. Those touchy love/hate moments between mother and daughter...sigh. We love each other, but hate having each other under our skins. Last night I had another run-in with her about preparing for ballet camp. I've been in a foul stupor this entire week and today I snapped. Erin is refusing to do anything physical and I am *p.o.'d* at her *and* the cancer craters in my body.

I think it's reasonable that she should be exercising and dancing, preparing for the very expensive two-week ballet camp I introduced her to, encouraged her to audition for, and for which I am paying. After getting accepted by the prestigious BYU summer dance program, her part of the bargain with us was to be prepared when she went. She agreed. That is reasonable.

She's not doing anything but sleeping in, painting her toenails, and watching *The Price Is Right* while eating lightly browned and buttered toast. And she's only doing that because I dynamite her out of bed at 10 a.m.

She must be a princess.

Just to be sure, the next time she leaves to hang out with friends, I'll slip eighteen more Serta Perfect Sleepers on her pillow-top twin and slide a Jolly Green Giant frozen petite pea under the pile. Ho Ho Ho. That way, when she feels the uncomfortable lump on her back, it will propel her out of bed before brunch. When that occurs, I'll beg her forgiveness and offer my obeisance.

How many times did our mothers say *I hope that someday you have a darling child just like you* or *Someday you'll understand* or *Just you wait* or, in the case of really patient mothers like mine, just one loud, long, drawn-out *sigh*. Payback is not so sweet when you're behind the "accounts receivable" parental desk.

Is it just me, or is the "no preparation method" wise for Erin's strenuous competitive camp? At 16, I was acting, singing, and dancing at the Ricks College summer scholars' academy, surrounded by beautiful, mysterious, willowy prima donnas not-so-subtly competing for center stage. Normally a big frog in the little pond of Blackfoot, it was tough to suddenly become lost in the crowd, one of many scummy *little* toads chasing a few measly flies around a *big* pond. It's so easy to lose yourself in bigger ponds and drown.

This daughter of mine is a lovely young woman blessed with all the talents she needs for the world. She is privileged to have the classics in her life and the time to pursue them. She could win scholarships to universities if she chose to do so. She is a *very* gifted dancer. She pulls you into the music and movement until it takes your breath away and makes you weep.

What makes me weep now is that we didn't see Malevolent the Dark Fairy coming, wand in hand, to strike our princess with such lethargy. It enrages me that my gifted daughter is wasting today in sloppiness, apathy, fears, and Bob Barker.

If I had the chance, I'd grab my youthful body back in a Blackfoot minute and *pas de bourree (yes, potty-boo-ray)* off in a tutu. I'd keep my old brain, though; even if the price is forgetting where I laid my leotard. I wouldn't want a life encore with a teenage brain. The wiseguy who said youth is wasted on the young must have been the mother of a teenage ballerina.

Oh, don't accuse me. I don't need to live vicariously through her; I've been a ballerina, a drill teamer, a folk dancer, a Funky Chicken. I'm over it. Most days.

But today I slammed my bedroom door against all this and ate my toast in solitary confinement. If she's a princess, I must be a queen. Oh, yeah.

Later that afternoon, I told her that she couldn't leave for our 7 p.m. church youth activity until her homework was done and dinner eaten, but she grabbed her backpack and left with Mark and Mikey, defiantly, at 5 p.m. Group study? Yeah, right. Burger King study is more like it.

After Princess left in a huff and Father of Princess just sat staring into his chicken bones and the cold skin of his baked potato, I snapped. I saved my real snappage until the rest of our royal offspring were out of sight, so as not to scare them. I yelled at the King in frustration, in wicked PMS, in motherhood, in cancer spots, threw three days' worth of Seattle Times into the recycling bin, and, to beat it all, picked up my half-full (no, half-empty!) glass of cranberry juice and, without thinking, threw it across the back wall of the kitchen in an amazing red spray of temper.

Wow, I'd never done that before! I surprised myself.

Father of Princess still did not say a word, hoping, I suppose, though I don't know for sure because he didn't speak, that I would calm down and let steam come out of my ears instead of my mouth. Nay, but I stalked upstairs, grabbed my purse, and left the house, slamming the door behind me. I didn't know where I was going. I was wearing my old, floppy, pink bedroom slippers and no make-up—but I went.

I went lost.

I just drove. Without seeing the forest *or* the trees *or* dropping any bread crumbs *or* stopping to smell the roses I somehow ended up in Fall City and then onto the freeway to North Bend. Hmmm. OK. "Green, Green, it's green, they say, on the far side of the hill; Green, Green, I'm goin' away to where the grass is greener still," as the New Christy Minstrels used to sing.

Wherever you head, there you end up, green or not. But where was I? The landscape was familiar. I was not.

Taking a wild left, my Astro van suddenly decided to go to the North Bend Outlet Mall. Since I wasn't wearing a speck of make-up, my old, floppy, pink bedroom slippers first took me into the Prestige Make-Up Boutique. I had *never* gone out in public without make-up or public façade or baseball cap hiding greasy hair. And, oh, don't forget my slimy mind. The Queen had gone with all uglies exposed, AWOL incognito.

I purchased the Prestigious basics—mascara, eyeliner, blush, and eyebrow pencil. Can't be having no eyebrows in this state of mind. Eyebrows fall off your face on your fortieth birthday; mothers can fall off the wagon of queenly propriety at any moment before or after that. And there's no make-up that makes up for that.

I grabbed a Prestigious hairbrush and asked the clerk, who was curious about my scary appearance and nervous about my scary attitude, the most burning question on my mind. Wait, I lie. The most burning question on my mind: was *What would happen if I kept driving to North Boston instead of just stopping here in North Bend?*

So, being sensitive to her jitters, I asked her my second most burning question, "Could you please tell me where the nearest motel is?"

"Um...I don't know," she said, staring up at my no-eyebrow glare. Off with her head. But I hadn't purchased a Prestigious tool for that.

The car was a delightful place to put on make-up. Every queen should use the rear-view mirror. There are homeless women all over America who *do* use a rear-view mirror every day since it's in the middle of their bedroom, but that fact did not shame me out of my pity party.

Mindlessly, my Prestigious hairbrush scraped my dirty, messy mass into a very stylish ponytail. Oh, cool, reminds me of eighth grade. Oh, I looked much better, now that my crowning glory was styled. All the beauty books you could ever desire from the Weekly Reader Book Club exhorted us to "Keep your hair spanking clean because, after all, it's a woman's crowning glory." What is "spanking" clean? Crowning glory? Speaking of crowns, where was mine today?

Since I had run away mostly barefooted, my old, floppy, pink bedroom slippers took me next to the Bass Shoe Outlet and together we picked out a great pair of summer canvas Mary Janes that almost fit. No glass slippers in sight. Continuing our impulsive spree, we grabbed two pairs of linen pants (one of them was three sizes too big, but I liked the fabric), two shirts, and a straw hat—commemorating the last straw that broke my back an hour earlier. It was very heady, cathartic even, to use my credit card indiscriminately for the first time without thinking about the consequences. Wild emotional spending was way more fun than banging my head against an unpadded wall. But debt with high interest is much more dangerous than an unpadded wall, though that is not what we consider before our sprees. *Tomorrow is another day,* Scarlett O'Hara philosophizes every time you push her into your VCR. She'll say it every day if you need her to.

After the Straw Hat Episode, the hunger from having worked so hard at being miserable was gnawing a royal hole in my stomach, so I stopped for a deluxe something or other. Soggy toilet paper fast food. Disgusting—perfectly befitting my mood.

Wiping my mouth on my sleeve, I threw my deluxe wrapper, napkins, and paper cup with ice on the floor of the van, then threw my to-go sack on top of it all. Why, that felt great! I paused for a moment to analyze this new scientific experiment. Thesis: How does the rest of my family feel (or don't feel, is more like it) when they drop their stuff any-old-where for the queen to pick up? Conclusion: It would feel pretty darn good to have someone else clean up your messes!

I found the address of the North Bend Motel in the pay phone Yellow Pages and drove around and around the tiny dorp of a town until I found it. As a man's home is his castle, so does the North Bend Motel become a woman's castle when she is under certain spells.

Spell C-H-E-A-P. For $36 plus tax I could spend the night in solitary, peaceful bliss watching the Sonics/Jazz basketball game we had anticipated viewing as a family, without being forced to watch any of my Tormentors, Dungeon Keepers or their Royal Messes. I didn't want to miss this tournament game, so hey, in my North Bend castle I could make messes of my own, walk away tomorrow since it's another day, and have someone else clean up behind me! Then I *would* feel like a queen.

I sat in the car staring at *Welcome Vacancy* on the old North Bend Motel marquee for 86 minutes. I stared until the North Bend Motel stopped looking like a castle. I stared until it started looking like what it was—no eyebrows on the face of thin luxury.

If I stayed overnight, it would be essential to explain my absence to the Royal Family. The two little Princes would have to know I was OK before I crashed here, since they were still young enough to worry if Mommy, their sad queen, didn't come home for bedtime prayers. The oldest Prince would be worried, too, as he loved the kingdom to always be peaceful. But Princess might hope Mommy was gobbled up by some scaly cave-dweller. That's how normal daughters feel when mothers are buried subcutaneously like a tick under young skin—except the tick feels like a dragon.

The King would have to fix the strawberries for the special youth-group breakfast tomorrow morning. That would mean the queen would have to call anyway and give a long explanation and description about berry fixing, when she didn't want to speak to him until the Royal Cows came home to moo at the Royal Flying Pigs.

The dilemma—knowing you'll feel horrid if you stay away versus knowing that if you go home you'll find the family the same and go to bed angry and frustrated—would make you sick. But I had sickened myself by now anyway, so what would be the difference?

Well, there is a difference, Scarlett, and, duh, it doesn't have to start tomorrow.

It took living through my 30s to learn a thing or two and to work through most of my baggage: abuse by a family "friend," the chronic illness of fibromyalgia, the death of my mother, forgotten dreams, blah, blah, blah…the regular list of stuff that everybody must overcome and learn from. The rage, the mistrust, the restlessness, the withdrawal, the flights—I had learned to handle it and get over it and get on without it, without so much drama. Or so I thought. Packing up baggage now to run away again, even for one night, would be a huge setback—a slap, a nose-thumbing to the victories I'd achieved. Queens don't treat themselves or their families like that.

No more catching my breath for a couple days without explanation. No more running away. Wherever you run to, there you end up, with all your bags flubbering along behind.

You cannot outrun your baggage.

You can unpack it, sort the contents, and toss stuff out. You can store empty bags in a dark corner of your closet, in the garage, or you can give them away to the thrift store. But trying to run away with flubbering baggage dogging your every step is impossible. I had to face the royal chamber music—the more people you keep in a house, even in the deepest love, the more baggage there will be.

So I sat staring at *Welcome Vacancy* for 86 long minutes until I understood that it was pointing not at this little old run down motel...but at my brain.

Distantly, the women I admire took shape in my thoughts. Their identities were fixed firmly in their minds and hearts and spirits. They knew who they were—just ordinary women who had conquered some of their own dark inner queendoms one glass of cranberry juice at a time. They were women like my mother and my grandmothers, who never spoke of their baggage aloud to me, but I know now that they set some aside to get on with living joyful lives. They were women like my best girlfriends, who do confide aloud. They were the women at the BYU Women's Conference every year who I embraced as role models. You listened with every fiber of your being as these fellow warriors recounted their own quests and what worked for them. You saw strong spirits shining through modest clothes, minimal make-up, and slightly outdated hairdos. You saw moral victories radiating in their countenances; victories over the adversities, the enticements, the vanities of this world. I am talking *queens*.

Ironically, after 86 minutes with *Welcome Vacancy* staring me full in the face, my window of remembrance opened to a shining, stunning fact. At those very women's conferences, for years, I had read aloud my own poetry to audiences of women hungry for spiritual support. We were all ordinary soldiers struggling for personal, private victories. They had listened to what *I*, a flawed and very average queen-in-the-making, offered about the ebb and flow of daily struggles.

Some days I forget I will have daily struggles.

No, an impulsive outlet shopping spree would have been over-the-top for my role models and sickening in its distractibility. The women I admire were beyond old, floppy, pink bedroom slippers on the loose. They wouldn't stay here overnight, nor would they have run away in the first place. Thanks anyway, old North Bend Motel.

They would not have tossed their cranberry juice. They might not have judged their Princesses so harshly. (But I'm not positive about that one.) I'm not sure what they would think when staring at a *Welcome Vacancy* sign. But, then again, maybe I am.

In the spring of the year I turned 16, I lost a popular election at my high school in the race for school mascot. Positioned between four cheerleaders, the mascot wore a cutesy, shorty green outfit and a humungous paper maché horse head. We were the Broncos, the Mighty, Mighty Broncos. I, and others, thought the mascot was the darling of the school.

Devastated at the victory dance when my opponent's name was called out instead of mine, I kept smiling until midnight and the dance ended. Then two friends and I, Kelly and Larry, got in my big family Buick and went for a drive rather than going home. *Welcome Vacancy.* I needed to run away.

We were good kids and just three friends. No booze, no drugs, no hanky-panky in the back seat. We just drove, trying to find the hill on the Fort Hall Indian reservation where we knew, from the top, we could see for a hundred miles, catching the lights of three small Idaho cities. I needed some glitter.

We drove in search of something. We weren't sure what. We just went. We went lost. We thought we never found what we were looking for.

Two and a half hours past my curfew, without calling home; when I got in at 3 a.m., Dad was pacing the floor. He'd just come home from searching for me in his old Ford pickup, wondering where my bruised, broken, bloody body might be lying. Mom was too sad and angry to get up and welcome home the prodigal daughter. I could not understand, then, Dad's hopeful, aimless searching for me when he didn't even know where I had gone.

I could see the grief leave his eyes and the relief settle in as I walked through the back door to our family room. He noticed the grief in my own eyes at what I perceived, at 16, to have been an immeasurable loss—the false promise of cutesy, shorty green under a paper maché horse head.

I got no punishment from them. I just saw *Welcome home, princess* in their eyes the next day; forgiveness, and some other essence that I was too young and self-absorbed to notice in my mother's quiet warrior countenance. I don't remember apologizing for scaring my parents, causing such worry, pushing *them* to run away to who-knows-where. They never tried to scratch me out from under their skin.

Now, after loving a husband and four children, I understand what my parents felt. I understand what my role models decide when staring at tempting signs: shut out the glowing *Welcome Vacancy* and head home. I understand the real job of sister warriors. I understand what truly constitutes an immeasurable loss.

What a strange occurrence, then—like déjà vu—to see my parents' emotions from long ago in the eyes and bodies of my spouse and children as I walked through the door to our family room after running away to the North Bend Motel. They saw the same emotions in me.

We seek for each other because we love each other, even though we don't exactly know where to look on those long roads that take us away. I understand Dad's searching now, and I'm grateful.

Because I've been 16 for 34 years, I know that choosing queenly means choosing wisely. The Royal Decree is thus: I like where I am now. I like where I'm going. I don't want to return to my sixteenth summer and live it all over again, even though the desire to go back and look deep into the eyes of my past sometimes pulls hard.

OK, accuse me then, I'm not over it—I still love to dance. Is there anyone who doesn't want to dance again? I'd still love to get back up in toe shoes and find my *pirouettes*. And they're not in the cookie aisle.

So it's my daughter's turn. Erin can do it for herself. She is a talented, capable ballerina, eloquently expressive. I would never squish her into my toe shoes.

I apologized to my family for scaring them and causing them such worry. I gave heartfelt obeisance by holding their warm little bodies as I begged their forgiveness. The abysmal fairy tale was ancient history.

I got home just in time to clean up my burger garbage from the van; in time to scrub the cranberry juice off the wall before it set a stain so deep I had to repaint; in time to clean up my own mess. (Even though I had tired myself out practicing misery and wishing the King would clean it to apologize for his part in the Royal Uproar.) I cleaned it all up before watching the Jazz behead the Sonics by 35 points in Game Six.

Some critics didn't think we could do it.

And we loved happily ever after. Stacks and stacks of lumpy mattresses.

I've Been 16 for 34 Years - BoomerTweener

Where's your bringin' ups? Were you born in a barn?
            -Myrtle and Loren Martin

Chicken Fat
2005

Pop Quiz:
1. In 1962, when President John F. Kennedy formed the President's Council on Physical Fitness, the official theme song was:
    a. "Plum Buns"
    b. "Chicken Fat"
    c. "Sticky Rice is Mighty Nice"

If you paid attention to the title of this essay, you guessed "b." That's correct!

Eons ago in a galaxy far, far away...there was *Chicken Fat. "Touch down, every morning...Ten times! Now and then...Go, you, Chicken Fat, go!"* You may have heard this groovy ditty every single day as your entire elementary school student body performed morning P.E. for 6½ minutes in the gym. (Unless you grew up in California, where you totally missed out, because you pedaled a bike to school or steeple-chased over neighborhood hedges, escaping bullies.)

Distributed to thousands of grade schools, yes, almost every grade school across this, our great nation, millions of us American children made this routine the most popular of all youth programs in the **history of the world**, as we actually **enjoyed** exercising. With our pedal pushers under petticoats under full skirts, or in our Beaver Cleaver button-downs, we sweated. **And** we sang along with Robert Preston..."*Give that chicken fat back to the chicken, and don't be chicken again...*" More soul-stirring than "Where Have All The Flowers Gone?" as harmonized by the Kingston Trio, and an anthem perkier than "Hair" as vocalized by the Cowsills, we sang *Chicken Fat*..

    I'm gaining on Seabiscuit, running effortlessly on my two middle-age legs, side by side with him around the soft track at Emerald Downs. No jockey on his back, it's a game between horse and woman. He's hugging the rail, making me swing wide. But I edge up. We come head to head. I look at him out of the corner of my eye.
    "Wun, Gwamma! Wun like da wind!"
    Sydney's voice is a figment of my feeble imagination as I sweat on the treadmill. My 2-year-old granddaughter loves to run and to boss—like some of the rest of us. The boring white wall three feet in front of me and the "Be Safe On The Treadmill" poster fade from view as I return to Seabiscuit.
    Flank to flank we run. His flanks are tightly muscled, rippling. Mine are not, rippling. Mine possess chicken fat. Little NeyNey cheers me on. OK, Syd, I'm running like the wind.
    The Biscuit turns his head to give me that *look*, the one we adored in his movie. With Red Pollard (Toby Maguire) on his back, Seabiscuit gives that *look* to his opponents right before he cranks it up and gallops off in turbo speed, when everyone believes he's defeated. *Just try to catch me!* I'm ready to give Biscuit a taste of his own oats, my own *look*, because I am going to win this footrace. And because I am the boss of my own...reality? Neigh.

    It's my imaginary world that must clinch this win, because, in reality, I'm coming up on 2.5 miles on the treadmill at the "Y" without the big cooling fan. Sweating like a pig, not because the Biscuit and I are locked in fierce historical combat, but because some real-life woman next to me adjusted the fan to pour directly on her. I must get into my right brain to finish this day of marathon training.
    Inspired by the idea of exercise and JFK, (and not my 1962 second-grade thighs) Meredith Wilson plunked himself down right after writing *The Music Man* and *The Unsinkable Molly Brown* and "Till There Was You" (a song The Beatles loved enough to record) and wrote "The Youth Fitness Song" reverently known as *Chicken Fat*. Not knowing JFK or Mr. Wilson personally, I cannot guarantee there is no secret government code embedded in these lyrics for all of us to obey this very second! (You are getting sleepy...very sleepy...)

Tune out the sweat, tune out the fatigue, the cellulite, the broken sesamoid bone in my right foot, tune out the 20 years of fibromyalgia. Just as I tune back into Seabiscuit with my demoralizing *look*, Sydney's voice pipes up again.

"Wun, Gwamma!"

I am, sweetheart, I am.

"Wun like Spotty da pony!"

The Biscuit vision instantly crumbles, as suddenly I trail a little fat black-spotted rump trotting down the track. Spotty the pony has me by a Shetland's length. I stumble along behind, whipped in the face by his shaggy black tail.

I giggle out loud. Treadmill woman next to me looks over, wishing she was having as much fun as me. I tune into her movement, turn my head, and give her the *look* I was saving for Seabiscuit. She jerks back, re-memorizing our yellow "Be Safe On The Treadmill" poster.

Thanks, little NeyNey, and thanks for being brave enough this year to ride your first real live Party Pony named Spotty. Thanks to you I've crushed this treadmill woman...even though Spotty's winning by a rump.

Hmmm, thinking of cute little things...where are you, Davey Jones? As every cool preteen with a mad crush knows, before you were a Monkee, hey, hey, you were a jockey. Where are you when I need you most? Only you can help me figure out how to beat Spotty. I giggle again.

Because my right brain simmers wide open; slowly gurgling up from the depths of my memory pops a tantalizing dumpling in hot oil...*Chicken Fat*. And from this stew-y muse I sing the only phrase I can recall... "*Touch down, every morning...Ten times! Now and then...hmmm...hmmmm...hmmmm... Go, you, Chicken Fat, go!*" Is it "*now and then*" or "*not just now and then*"...

"What is that? What is that? What do you keep...chanting?" Treadmill woman cries out at me in pain.

"*Chicken Fat.* Oh, did I sing that out loud? Oh! '*No, don't be chicken again!*' You mean...that?" Treadmill woman—why, she must be from California!—has nevertheless inspired me with another piece of the lyric puzzle by her vigorous response to my *Chicken* croonings.

She wavers, shrinks, gouging at buttons to start her cool down.

My mileage reads 4.08 before Mackenzie's voice interrupts the *Chicken Fat* humming in my right brain.

"Go, Gwandma, go!"
Come on, girls, I'm going already.
"Don' you tell me your pwoblems!" she barks in her most serious 3-year-old voice. Mackenzie leans forward, clapping her little palms together at my thighs before she falls in a heap with sister Sydney, laughing hysterically as toddlers do, a lot.

The girls float away together as my vision yanks me into an outdoor stadium. I glide in purple sport top and black running shorts, visor pulled low on my forehead. My opponents will not read my eyes. I lead the pack in the USA Track and Field 5000K Championship. Six Kenyans in yellow and green uniforms are hot on my heels; winded, but present enough to wonder how-in-the-heck this young little BoomerTweener granny from Washington has enough wind to cripple them, the best distance runners in the world. The Kenyans are followed by a motley crew of competitors: grannies, grandpas, cross-country-running teens, construction workers, politicians, oil and gas magnates, that college professor who gave me a D in botany lab, and commuters on scooters. They all sweat. I run smoothly in first place, studying my fingernails on the last lap. Hmmmm, there's a hangnail. But not wanting to totally demoralize the pack, I focus on the race.

Now we all run on the plains of Kenya. Sinewy brown legs, muscular white legs, some lean and strong, some chicken fatty and feeble, all pound the dirt trail behind me. My aging Northwest sun-deprived kneecaps run like the wind. The oil and gas magnates are plucked like marshmallows off a campfire stick by crocodiles concealed in four inches of mud on the trail. The commuters on scooters bog down in sand and almost get gobbled up by lions; until they're inadvertently saved by the politicians, who, ignoring the good trail, straggle off in the opposite direction with a large pride following behind. A roar and a burp and life is good again for the rest of us. I cross the finish line in first place, bend over with dignity to receive my medal from Meryl Streep and Winston Churchill, who utter harmoniously in authentic British accents, "Nevah, nevah, nevah give up!" and I just have to giggle out loud again.

California treadmill woman next to me, plucking away every particle of cool air in the place, can't take me any more.

She puts on the brakes as I glide past her to 4.47 miles, and she stumbles away without readjusting our fan. Thanks, sistah.

"... not just...now and thennnnnn...Give that chicken fat back to the chicken, and don't be chicken again!" Don't fight that the words and tune to *Chicken Fat* are stuck in your head for weeks. Better to have *Chicken Fat* on your mind than on your thighs.

OK, almost done. Going to five miles today in training for my first marathon. My husband beat prostate cancer in January and I turn 50 this year. We're celebrating. What better reasons to take on a horrendous new adventure? We'll run with two of our sons for "Team Oli," the family team. We're running to celebrate, to lengthen our stride, to see if we can finish, to set a pace, to be crazed and racked and rumbled. Why, oh why? Remind me why I'm doing this. Why?

Why do we go to the moon? Why do we climb Mount Everest? Why do we keep eating Twinkies? Because it's there—the road is always there. The end is tempting and delicious.

Nick, our oldest, experienced his first marathon last year with his wife. As I sat with their toddler son while they ran the race, I watched, inspired by the motley crew of runners crossing the finish line—tall ones, short ones, fat and thin, some were crying, some had grins, super young, super old, sweat pants, cargo shorts, dress socks, sport socks, old shoes, new, tiny running shorts, and sport bras, too. Sounds like a Dr. Seuss race. It was, it totally was.

I scrutinized these screwballs approaching the big finish line, cheered when my kids came in together, lifted my grandson over the orange mesh barrier to them, then sniveled tears of joy as they all crossed the finish line as one. Carried away by this stirring spectacle, I naively thought *Hey, if they all can do this, I can do this, too.*

Our third child, K.C., is training for this new adventure with us. Our boys will barely break in new shoes and a sweat, and they'll beat us, me, by hours. K.C. calls what I do "shuffling." That's OK, as long as I beat the Kenyans and the commuters. Shuffling like a dumpling...

"Come to me, endorphins!"

Nick sent us a good training book and I'm using it religiously. In his book, *Marathon*, Jeff Galloway, who has run a bazillion marathons, gives you tips to train and race with. He maintains that getting into your right brain is important so you don't dwell on the icky stuff like broken bones and cancer. Though he doesn't mention training to *Chicken Fat* in his book, he does offer "dirty tricks" and words of encouragement to use, like *"I'm getting smoother and stronger!"* or *"Relax, power, glide!"* to shout silently at yourself when the going gets tough. My favorite so far is *"Come to me, endorphins!"*

Sometimes they do, sometimes they don't.

Pounding down the trail to the 5 mile finish...focus! I'm riding bareback on my gray Arabian gelding, Ramah, in my running togs; wearing bunny slippers on my feet, bearing a frosty backpack puffy with fudgesicles. We trot along in the sunshine next to the Kenyans as I call out with a smile..."*Relax, power, glide!"*

They do not.

I offer fudgesicles. "They're getting smoother and creamier and colder and yummier!" I try to coax them to a nibble. They refuse. Well then, how about a dumpling? No? That's OK. I squeeze Ramah's smooth sides with my bare legs in bunny slippers, slurp my fudgesicle, trot off into the sunset, chanting my mantra on the road to the bare white wall...

"*Go you chicken fat, go away! Go, you chicken fat, go!"*
"*Go, Gwamma, go!"*
"Wun like fuzzy bunnies!"

Run like Chicken Fat!

COWS—When they butter your bread, it's OK that they smell.
    -old German farmer saying

Never kick a cow chip on a hot day.
-Will Rogers

Don't try to squish 5 pounds of crap into a 3 pound sack; you'll get stuff all over.
-Kim A. Nelson's dad

"Hope" is a magpie eating road kill—it hops to the shoulder of the road, but shuffles right back again in a never-ending dance. It is never crushed by speeding cars. It is never discouraged from dining on dead rabbits.
-Julie J. Oliver

**30 Rules
For Living in Idaho**
2006

Dear Sue,

You asked me to tell you how to live in Idaho. Are you sure you don't want to move back? Alright then, you better stay there forever. Don't make anyone else weep at your going. I hate saying goodbye to friends.

I'll come visit you. I've been persuaded by these 30 reasons. I'll feel right at home again.

30 simple things you need to do:

1. Go barefoot...two cautions...
    A. Do not step on rusty nails.
    B. Do not wear flip flops out in the snow. Folks will think you're from California. Plus, your feet will get cold. And...this year they stopped serving barefooters at Flying J Truck Stop Café!

2. Wear fur in the winter—especially if it's coyote. Idahoans understand. They won't hate you or squirt red paint or ketchup on you. Furs are very warm. Ask the coyotes. A woman in a coyote coat is helpful to sheep farmers and anyone who loves their house pets. (We just lost our fifth cat to them—coyotes, that is, not women in fur. And on Monday, a pack of coyotes tried to eat my dogs for lunch! I fought them off with our red garden shovel. I am not making this up.)

3. Know your bugs. Potato beetles are not pill bugs and vice versa. City slickers call pill bugs potato bugs and think they're totally right. You are not a fool when you get your bugs straight.

4. Why is Idaho called *The Gem State*? Yes, this is a pop quiz! Answer: because of spuds. (Or maybe opals or something shinier than spuds.) Some residents call potatoes *spuds*. Doesn't matter; be sure to eat both kinds—Idaho spuds *and* Idaho Spuds. They're both easy to find in your new state, but the vegetable kind are better with sour cream on them than the chocolate kind.

5. Then there's your wild asparagus. Capture it! Canal banks, ditch banks, creeksides, roadsides—*I Brake For Wild Asparagus*. Eat it fresh or freeze it. Don't overcook it. If you try to grow it in your garden, give it lots of water every day and be patient for fifteen years.

6. Wear creams—sunscreen, moisturizer, eye oil, lip balm, lots of everything. *Slather,* as cityfolk say. Since it's dry, dry, dry there, you will grow more wrinkles than me. Ha! Don't you want to move back now? If not, invest in a case of the dairy farmer's best friend—Bag Balm.

7. Speaking of Bag Balm…sing to cows. If you sing to them, they will come. They'll follow you. They want richer, cultured lives. The old saying should not be *curious as a cat,* but *curious as a cow*. From much personal experience I know that cows are more curious than cats. If you sing to them, cows will think you're mysterious. They will love you more.

8. Acquire new tools: snow shovel, riding lawn mower, binoculars, BB gun, apple cider press, wild turkey call, medium-size tractor, four-wheeler, fly strips, big horse syringe, chicken wire, weeding hoe (that's h-o-E), fishing pole, waders, hammock, slingshot.

9. Battle new varmints: carp, coyotes, skunks, starlings, weasels, porcupines, blow snakes, Jerusalem crickets, June bugs, rock chucks, (How much rock can a rock chuck chuck?) and city people moving out for fresh country air who become offended by the smells.

10. Embrace the new English language:
    A. *We come home from Walmart real tarred from our shoppin' spree.*
    B. *I like these ones over here, Dave, woncha buy 'em fer me?*
    C. *Oh my heck!*
    D. *Dave, yew kin pinch a penny sa dang hard, yew make Lincoln squeal.*
    E. *Gosh, forty, Dave, I jist love everrthin' in Idaho!*
    F. *Wull, fer fun, Dave...yew brung me a rock chuck coat!*
    G. *I ain't never had such a flippin' cool coat as this chucker here, Dave!*

11. Teach 4-H: gardening, flower arranging, sewing, cooking, home decorating, fashion grooming, dog grooming, financial management, knitting, rock chuck skinning, social etiquette—you're so good at everything! And kids need to learn these crucial skills. It gives their little text-message thumbs, and their mothers, a rest.

12. Use sagebrush. Incorporate it into your wedding flower arrangements. Stun Idahoans with this creativity and beauty and wild aromatherapy. They will love you for your good heart and good flowers, your business will grow; and thus, you'll never find yourself just *rollin' along like a tumblin' tumbleweed.*

13. Love magpies. If our black and white feathered friends didn't eat roadkill, we'd see squashed stuff nose-to-tail, up and down highways from Kellogg to Preston. People think magpies are trashy birds because they eat maggoty things. But magpies exude personality. They're exotic. Just love them. They're

bouncing back from West Nile disease, so if the cows don't need you much, sing to the birds! (Just not *Four and Twenty Blackbirds baked in a...*)

14. Know your roadkill. Black and white in Idaho is skunk; black and white in Washington is possum. (*Why did the chicken cross the road? To show the possum it could be done.*)

15. Give thanks. No neighborhood deer ripping branches off your apple trees for a midnight snack! No raccoons or black bears feasting in your garbage! Oh, maybe a stray dog or two nibbling on your house cat...or your week-old Pampers...wait, take a second look. Why, it's just a desperate coyote.

16. Water is a verb. Water, water, water! That baby pine tree we sent south with you needs a big gulp every day. Remember how our forest grows. Remember our friendship. (Cell phones are not the same as crying on a brown couch together over our children and our fibromyalgia.)

17. Call your friends "hon." This term of endearment belongs to you and sounds right. It makes your pals feel like sisters, nurtured and loved, warm and fuzzy. Idahoans like to feel fuzzy.

18. Don't ever hope the wind will stop blowing. Buy a little clear plastic hair bonnet at the local Grange. Plant a long row of tall trees on the side of your property. Can you say *windbreak? OOOOO-klahoma! Where the wind comes sweepin' down the plain...* Nope—Idaho.

19. Build a clothesline. See #18. Hang your laundry out to dry. It'll smell like the sun and the prairie and the cool morning breeze. Wear that fragrance and sleep in it. There's nothing better in the entire world. Forget that it's a "green" thing to do. Farm wives have lived this secret for 2,000 years.

I've Been 16 for 34 Years - BoomerTweener

20. Don't be surprised that you've become exotic. Unpack, sort and discard, duct tape a "free" sign on what you don't want and plunk it down on your curb. (Do you have a curb or a borrow pit?) You'll be the cool new neighbor. Plus, it's less stuff to dust.

21. Be comfortable. Wear your mom jeans. High fashion arrives in Idaho twenty years late.

22. Eat happy. Green Jell-O, garden beans, roast beef with gravy over mashed potatoes, creamed "new" potatoes and garden peas, homemade bread and ice cream and cake. Grow your own roast beef! Your neighbors will teach you how.

23. Check Dave for ticks. Evening walks through the sagebrush can be dangerous. To remove ticks: light a match, blow it out and touch the tick bum with the hot match head. Watch it square dance out of your skin. Use tweezers if you need to. It's amusing. Let Dave check you for ticks. Amu-u-using!

24. Don't cry until the wind stops blowing. See #18. If you must cry during breezes…check the corners of your eyes afterwards because you'll have made mud pies there.

25. Wash your car = make it rain. A shiny car produces sprinkles, thus happier asparagus. Sprinkles + dust in the wind = scum car. And people finger-scrawling across your windows "wash me!"

26. Wave at your neighbors. They'll wave back.

27. Buy a horse. Ride him down the block at noon to get your mail. Ride him into the sunset. Ride him to the store for bread and a gallon of milk; you'll spend less and have more fun. (This is the answer to our nation's debt addiction, road rage, oil dependency, and paranoia to be "green.") To thank him for taking you great places, buy him some Butter Mints

28. Watch the sunsets. You'll sigh every night in joy and amazement and peace.

29. Love Idaho. Anyone who won't find beauty in Idaho is too stubborn to look. Anyone who can't find beauty in Idaho is too proud to see. There is not a happier place on earth. The-Theme-Park-That-Must-Not-Be-Named-In-Front-Of-Small-Children is the *second* happiest place on earth.

30. Last of all, THERE IS BAD NEWS! Let go of all hope that you will ever receive free benefits from the Idaho Potato Museum in Blackfoot, whose motto is: *"Free taters for out-of-staters."*

No hour of life is wasted that is spent in the saddle.
-Winston Churchill

And in the end, it's not the years in your life that count, it's the life in your years.
      -Abraham Lincoln

Nearsighted
1967-68

A terrible tragedy happened to me before I ever turned 16. I got eyeglasses.

Mrs. Allen, my seventh-grade homeroom and English teacher, looked like the Wicked Witch of the West from the best movie of all time, *The Wizard of Oz*. Except her skin wasn't green. And her black hair was cut pixie short rather than scraggly scary. Her boyish hairdo contrasted starkly with her ultrafeminine way of dressing. We didn't appreciate then that Mrs. Allen was a sleek, chic Witch. It was so far beyond our comprehension. Today I can appreciate that her look was Audrey Hepburn meets the Wicked Witch on *Laugh-In*. Can you picture her?

As I slouched through two years of Blackfoot Junior High School, whether the weather was hot Indian summer or frigid Deep Freeze winter, Mrs. Allen wore sleeveless sheath dresses with matching 3-inch, pointy-toed pumps. Her shoes did not simply match the colors in her paisleyed, swirlied, crazy-60s-patterned knee-length dresses; no, incredibly, her shoes were covered with the exact same fabric as her sheaths. Where did she shop? Where could she possibly find outfits like that in Blackfoot, Idaho? Did she construct them herself? No one could fathom, no one could imagine.

Perhaps on her summer breaks she spent her days in exotic New York City getting haircuts and buying chichi couture. No one in my school could even pronounce the word couture. Not even our principal. We'd never heard of chichi. We might only guess that chichi was the name of Mr. Hughie's poodle.

Because she was the most dreaded entity at Blackfoot Junior High School, Mrs. Allen was too terrifying to approach with a shallow, nonessential, curiosity question like *who is your designer?* You can't just blurt out a question like that to a person like this. If you spread your fright out over many weeks, picking away at it like a crow in a corn patch, eventually you can devour the whole crop and ask the question you are curious about. But it's not healthy to be scared stiff all year.

So it remains a mystery to this day.

Mrs. Allen clickety-clacked briskly down the halls, scattering students left and right when they heard her coming. There were several slow unfortunates who she swooped down upon. Gum-chewing girls were made to bend over and spit out their big pink Bazooka bubble wads into very public trashcans. Quaking basketball stars, normally heroic, were made to stand up straight. Wrestling jocks tucked in their shirt tails while she tapped her paisley toes, unsmiling.

She clickety-clacked up and down between our classroom seats, commanding us to sit up straight, place our feet under our desks, or wash our hands before we picked up her precious literature books. She demanded our precious personal hygiene be as fastidious as our precious correct spelling words and the diagramming of our precious sloppy sentences.

In September 1967, the first month of my first year in junior high school, she offered to read aloud to us. Big sophisticated junior high school students were still read aloud to? Wasn't this the warm and fuzzy afternoon stuff of grade school? The thought of putting our heads down on our desks and showing any kind of vulnerability in her presence, or each other's, made each of us squirm inwardly. To squirm outwardly might cause a clickety-clack right on over to our personal desk space, which would cause the instantaneous eruption of premature white hairs from our tiny skulls just before our brains exploded. No gob of Dippity-do wanted to experience that. And yet we remembered with fondness the days when Mr. Reynolds and Mmes. Colson, Wilson, Burningham, Shoemaker, and right on back to our beloved first-grade teacher, Mrs. Chapman, taught us that, at 12:30 p.m., to be read to was the perfect respite after an excruciating lunch recess. In Groveland Elementary School, there was no shame at any age in putting heads down on desks.

In Mrs. Allen's class of big britches seventh-graders, no one was brave enough to raise her hand and admit that this idea would be a welcome reprieve from the normal terrors here. It would even be *fun,* after the excruciating promenade through halls full of sweaty, anxious youngsters, to arrive in a classroom kept captive by The Witch Who Reads Aloud. But we were old now.

No one dared admit that we missed our mommies reading aloud to us. Death before admitting that we missed our sixth-grade teachers reading aloud to us while we colored, rested, or daydreamed, gazing out the windows on green meadows across the road, at cows chewing their cud in neighboring pastures. We knew that was what Mrs. Allen saw when she watched us chonking our Bazooka—ungrateful, cud-chewing miniature bovine.

So no one finked. We were united in our stoicism.

But one day Mrs. Allen could stand it no longer and she held up the book *Where the Red Fern Grows* and snapped, "This is a classic story. How many of you have read it?" Only Linda E. timidly raised her hand, although there were actually thirteen of us who had read it. "If you were the least bit interested in hearing it I'd be willing to read twenty minutes every day aloud to you," she sniffed, and stood gazing out the window through her black-rimmed cat glasses, chin lifted like a prima ballerina on a stage full of second-rate corps dancers, "but none of you want me to read aloud." Then she sighed loudly.

This was our first clue that she might be human. It did not occur to us that by holding out we could drive her nuts in a most passive-aggressive way. It was this sigh of hers that finally broke us.

What passed through the class then was an answering sigh, a silent sigh of relief. A cosmic shiver. A collective tenderness rippled through the class like a lightning bolt made of a fresh strawberry Twizzler. A sweet shock, like when you first see the Wicked Witch of the East at her squashed end, an inadvertent, curly-toed demise beneath Dorothy's house. One wicked sister down, one to go.

Mrs. Allen remained poised, oblivious to our liberation and hers. Half-turned toward the window, her gaze suddenly locked on some unfortunate munchkin outside, late for class. She tapped on the glass, scowled and pointed at him, and he scurried inside. She regained her poignant pause, offering us a big double door of knocking opportunity. It was now or never, time to strike while the broom was parked, time to pitch our house down out of the stormy sky.

Thank heaven for Barry Smith's quavering voice. "Mrs. Allen?"

"Yes, Barry."

"I...I...I think we'd like to hear it."

"You would?" She squinted at him suspiciously through her lenses before sweeping her fierce frowny smile across the room to ensnare us all. "You all would?" Her voice rose in volume. Her lips found their way back to their familiar pursing after her question. Her head darted here and there around the room, searching for an assertion or a sister or a switch to twitch.

We nodded nervously as one, zombie-like.

"Well, why didn't you say so? Why didn't you speak up weeks earlier?" she demanded, the tiniest hint of a true smile playing around her smoker-puckered lips. Striding around behind her desk, she sat, opening her well-worn novel with satisfaction. "All right, we'll start into the first chapter," adding a bit shyly, "If you'd like to, you may put your heads down on your desks." Was she toying with us?

Our pride had been stripped weeks ago. Thirty-one heads hit thirty-one desktops. Defenseless before our Witch, we allowed her to captivate us with coon hounds. Ironically, here began the most serene moments of our junior high school days.

Unfortunately for me, I was very sick in seventh-grade with lots of swollen gland issues. I missed two spelling tests back to back and had to stay after school to make them up. Me and The Witch, alone together.

It's one thing to be hunting raccoons as a group. It's one thing to all sniffle silently on the same page. You'd think crying over dogs would bond you to the classroom menace, you'd even feel comfortable. But the thought of being alone with her still terrified me and there was not another student in my class, not even Barry Smith, who needed to make up those spelling tests. I was flying solo.

After the last bell of the day rang out with a dire note, I slunk back into my homeroom, shrinking into my desk like Dorothy looking for danger in the castle. Mrs. Allen clickety-clacked into the room and up and down my row; and I was trapped, trapped like a rat. Where was my bucket of water?

She carefully enunciated each spelling word before using it in a sentence. "Occasionally. Occasionally. She occasionally took the train to Madrid to watch the bullfights." Did Mrs. Allen read these sentences from the teacher's manual or did she pick them from her personal journal? Perhaps Madrid was a clue to the mystery of her shoes. Clickety-clack. Clickety-clack.

"That's a lovely watch you're wearing," she gently tapped the face of my cheap goldtone watch as she whooshed by in a vague mist of Tabu perfume.

"Th-thank you," I stammered, surprised by the compliment from my nemesis, surprised that she noticed I even owned an arm with warm skin on it. I always got 100 percent on spelling tests, without stress or study, but this particular afternoon I noticed a sweaty, white-knuckle grip on my yellow Ticonderoga No. 2.

She corrected my spelling tests at her desk while I made up another assignment, rewriting ten sentences from the blackboard, correcting the obvious grammatical mistakes she had placed there to trap me, trap me like a little girl with a tinder-dry scarecrow friend near fire. I'll get you, my pretty.

"Julie," she spoke sharply. "Are you squinting at the blackboard?"

"Um, no," my mouth automatically denied it before I could think of the correct response and I wriggled around to find some comfort. Do not expose yourself while alone with her. I stopped wriggling. I stopped squinting. Then I couldn't see. Had I been squinting? I sensed that to admit this weakness would cause great grief somewhere. "I...I don't think so."

"You were. You were squinting at the blackboard."

"Oh." What could I say? I was? I wasn't about to argue with her. "Um, yes?"

"I want you to go get your eyes checked immediately. Have your parents make an appointment for you and go see an eye doctor."

"OK, Mrs. Allen, I will."

"If you don't get your eyes checked in the next five days, I will make sure you see the school nurse next Wednesday."

"OK."

"I'm writing a note to your mother about this. See that she gets it."

"Yes, ma'am." Actually, I didn't say ma'am, although I wanted to. I was afraid to seem impertinent using that expression of respect. We don't say *ma'am* in Southeastern Idaho as far as I know, though we should have, for her. She probably would have like it. *Ma'am* is not a Blackfoot word.

That was Friday. I saw Dr. Hepworth on Saturday.

I didn't know I was legally blind. I really didn't know. I didn't know I couldn't see. Blurry was just the way of seeing that I was used to. One day you have clear vision and the next thing you know, you've been getting blurrier and blurrier without noticing that you're losing something precious.

I was fitted with my glasses on Tuesday after school, just missing the dreaded Wednesday deadline. As I stepped out of Dr. Hepworth's office, I had to look down to keep my balance. I saw that there was a blue carpet under my feet and a doorjamb to step through. I saw that there was concrete under my shoes. So this is what a sidewalk looks like! I saw that there were tiny gray, blue, and brown rocks strewn about the edges of the sidewalk. I didn't know such things existed down below. I thought *it's what they call gravel*. I saw puffy cumulus clouds overhead, huge and soft, racing away with the prairie breezes that blow down through the Snake River Valley. I saw a tiny black dog straining at the end of its brown leash, trying to pull its girl forward faster than she wanted to shuffle. Was that a cairn terrier? It looked an awful lot like Toto. I didn't know there was such a dog in Blackfoot. Carpet and clouds and cairns, oh my!

"I'm never gonna wear these things," I complained to my mother. Once we were in the green family Buick I took my new glasses off and snapped them into the hard-sided case Dr. Hepworth had given me. It was red with yellow paisley swirls. Mrs. Allen wore a red sheath covered with yellow paisley swirls. And, don't you know, she had high heels to match.

My world faded back to blurry, back to the sight I was used to. I was prejudiced against eyeglasses, a regular glasses bigot. My dad wore reading glasses. My mom wore black-and-white cat glasses all the time because she was nearsighted. They were almost like Mrs. Allen's. My oldest brother wore glasses, though he was no geek. Some of my classmates wore glasses and for years I had heard what the cool kids called the glasses kids. Overnight I was kidnapped into parents-geeks-and-four-eyes prison.

And because of my paisley case, things went from bad to horrendous—I was accessorized to match The Witch.

"They're stupid and I'm not gonna wear 'em."

I made Mrs. Allen so happy on Wednesday. She actually *smiled* at me when she peered down her nose at our class after the first period tardy bell rang. Every sidelong glance in the room swiveled at the edge of eyeballs toward me, wondering what was up. Here I am, friends, just an ugly monkey ready to fly at its master's bidding. Oh yes, I was wearing glasses today and The Witch had spotted my case.

My insecurities grew unruly, winning out over vision. Between every class I scurried, taking my oh-so-groovy brown tortoiseshell glasses off and hiding them in my Mrs. Allen Case, stuffed deep in the bottom of my macramé bag.

It took me one more week to realize that there were lots of things I had never seen before. One more week after that and you couldn't pry those puppies off my face.

It took thirty-four years after that to appreciate the fact that it was my nemesis who sharpened things up for me, making it possible for me to see with such clarity. I saw rocks, clouds, dogs, my friends, and that I was eating the school specialty, chili and a gigantic homemade cinnamon roll, for school lunch every Tuesday until I graduated from high school. Thelma the Good Witch made possible cool reading and writing stuff, wicked hard tests, and precious terrifying situations. While I was blind, I was totally unaware that I was missing out on such fine details.

It's funny—what you first think is a horrible problem turns out to be a blessing in disguise. Sometimes a house falling on your head can help you see things clearly.

Yep, a house plopped on your noggin from out of a stormy sky can make you more alive.

The pessimist sees difficulty in every opportunity. The optimist sees the opportunity in every difficulty.
-Winston Churchill

Terrible Phone Prank
1995

You never can be certain of what is *not* rattling easily around in your brain.

I need to discuss gray skies and chocolate and it just can't wait. I have to call Jeri right now. No! What? I cannot remember her telephone number!

Ohmygosh. My best friend of 22 years and today I cannot remember her phone number! I had to leave her two years ago and go away with my husband and kids to a different state for his work. That is no excuse. She is my best friend!

I know the area code and I thought I knew the prefix. It's the last four numbers that's the killer. 9155? I dial 9155 and get a busy signal. No, it's not 9155. That is my cousin's number.

Wait, *is* it 9155? Did I have the prefix correct? The prefix is 4-something. No, it's 8-something. Stop. That's the area code, not the prefix. The prefix...555—no that's the movies. Hold on! It's 325. No, that was my last prefix.

I've got it! Her number is 9144. No, that's my dentist's number. Who also happens to be my cousin's husband. I am not dialing that number and making a fool of myself with his receptionist. Besides, now I'm not sure of *that* prefix.

Dramatic irony. I can still remember the phone number from my babyhood. Sunset 5-2282. 785-2282. How easy is that? In the olden days, ugly numbers were prettied up with poetic words. It's the only number I ever had to memorize....yeah, when I was, like, 2.

Perhaps it's time to mine my planner for her number. No luck. Why didn't I write it down in my planner? Her address is there. I didn't write it down because I absolutely *knew* I would absolutely *never* forget her phone number, that's why. It's time to spend 75 cents and call information. It's not 75 cents anymore. Aargh! What is it now, $6.50? Cost is not an issue. It doesn't matter. I need to talk to Jeri *now*.

Break down and call information. Bad luck and incredulity! Her name and number isn't listed. When did this happen? What's up with this, US West? What's up with this, Miss Jeri?

So...no information saved in the planner, but ah ha! I wrote it down in my little address book next to the kitchen phone, didn't I? Yay! Save yourself from drowning by brain cramp.

Come here, little address book. It is gone! Search and search in the box next to our phone, through new bills, outdated wedding invitations, scraps of old phone messages, and expired grocery coupons. Fake organizer! Lethal procrastinator! Someone should clean this space out. Heckfire! Who took my little address book? I hate it when this happens. Pet peeve! I leave pens and pencils, scissors, tape and address books where we can all use them, and someone in this house takes them and doesn't return them!!! I hate that!!! Aargh! (Was it me?)

Didn't Mom always say *a place for everything and everything in its place*? We all know that works. I had a place in my brain for Jeri's phone number, but her number is not in its place.

I am home alone. So I scream. A long, loud primal scream. It hurts my throat. But I feel better.

Back upstairs I ransack my mind again like I ransacked my phone box. Someone should really clean out my mind space. I know it's not 9155, but it's 91...something, 91...something. I try 9155 one more time.

"Mornin'," says a husky voice.

Maybe she has a cold. "Uh, Jeri?" This is not Jeri. The bad news—it's not her husband either. I do not think fast. How not to embarrass myself with this complete stranger? I'm back in Mr. Taylor's ninth-grade math class after flunking a test full of negative numbers.

"No, this is Jan. Jerry's just left for work."

Long pause. Talk about being in a different state. Am I in the Twilight Zone? All I can stutter is, "Uh...uh... Jan, are you watching the kids for Jeri?"

"What kids?"

OK, now for the good news—one number down, a gazillion to go. Where's Mr. Taylor and his ability with statistics or probability and junk when you need him? I'm not sure if this Jan person is a man or a woman. It could be Pat from *Saturday Night Live*. I will not get out of this gracefully. "Um...you didn't know Jeri has three kids?"

"Wha...? He don't have three kids..."

Yep, I'm sure now that I can cross this multiple choice answer off my test, except I can't remember what number I just dialed. My dilemma at not finding Jeri reaches a zenith that I just cannot control. So, I cannot resist. "Not that you know of, anyway. You better ask him about it when he comes home from work tonight."

Jan grunts, "What the..."

"Um, Jan, while I have you on the phone...is your refrigerator running?" As I hang up, I can hear Jan starting to curse me and I'm *still* not sure if Jan is a man or a woman. I'm really sorry, Jan. And I mean that in the most sincere way.

Wait for my pounding heart to slow down before trying another prefix with the good old standby 9155. Barb and Karen's answering machine. I know Barb and Karen as well as I know Jan.

Quick, hang up! No more Twilight Zones for me, thank you very much. I haven't phone-pranked for the past 40 years. I knew it wasn't 9155. Trust your first impression, kid. Hmmm...what number did I just dial to get Barb and Karen? Pop quiz. Oh, yeah... I try a new area code, a totally new prefix, and 9144.

"Yes?"

Slam the phone down truly, madly, deeply, and glance over my shoulder. I'm creeping myself out. I'm keeping my long-distance company in business.

Oh, wait! Happy day! It's all coming back to me now! Must have been the shock therapy I just gave myself. It *is* 9144. Could it be 9144? That sounds so familiar. OK, I'll try it one more time with a different prefix. Ring. Ring. Ring.

"Good Morning!" she trills. Oh, my stars, it's Jeri's number *and* my cousin-dentist's number, too! Thank you, Phone Fairy. Thank you, Tooth Fairy.

Only Jeri answers the phone this way, always—*Good Morning!*—in the happiest voice imaginable. You'd swear you were getting on a ride at Disneyland.

"Good morning! How *are* you?" I trill back. What a relief, I'm not senile after all.

"Oh, fine. Gosh, I missed you. I wanted to talk to you in the store the other day but you got away before I could catch you," says Jeri.

What? Horror! Back into the Twilight Zone I fall.

"You don't recognize my voice?!!! You don't know it's me?! Oh, my gosh, it's happened!" I croak in pain.

"Oh, nooooo! Hiiiiii!!!!!" Jeri sings. "This other girl just called me and told me she had to hang up, but she'd call me right back. She's new and I don't know her voice yet."

"Yes, but you didn't recognize *my* voice!" I whine.

"Oh, no! I'm awful!" she laughs, apologizing.

"But guess what? I couldn't remember your phone number. I called a wrong number, then you weren't listed, and then I thought I remembered...then I did, after many tries, and...wait a minute, I have to write it down right now before I forget it. Oh, where's my pen?" I can't find a pen that writes. I throw things around my nightstand. "And then you didn't recognize my voice! We've been apart too long. It's time for a visit!"

"You are so right. I know it's you! I wasn't expecting you to call me. What a surprise! How *are* you?" she starts over.

"I'm fine. Are we that old? Will we forget again? This was traumatic. I don't want this to happen again!"

"Me neither. How scary."

And then, suddenly, we are back to normal, taking up where we left off weeks ago, like best friends do; telling how we love our little darlings, our husbands, empathizing over gray skies, chocolate, and each other. But, I feel six new gray hairs growing from my temples as 84 chestnut hairs cascade off my scalp. This harrowing incident was like driving Dad's old Ford pick-up over the narrow People's Canal bridge with my learner's permit at 14 years of age—terrified I'd drive us all over the brink and into cold rushing water, but not slowing down to shift gears for fear I'd stall.

I'm *certain* I will never forget this traumatic phone experience, but you never can tell, so never say never. After all of today's new trauma, I have to admit—you never can tell which state you're really in when you think you're only one state apart.

9144, 9144, 9144, 9144...now *where* did I just put that pen? 9044, 9044, 9044....

Intuition and hunches are usually lurking just below your conscious level, so trust your gut. Unless it's filled with antipasto, lasagna, salad, garlic bread, gelato, and pecan pie.
                              -Julie J. Oliver

Fleeting
January 20, 2006

    The high spot of my day—the very happiest—was spotting a ladybug crawling on my bedroom carpet. I was vacuuming.
    At the exact same time I saw it, I inadvertently sucked it up in the vacuum.
    Just like that, ladybug was gone with the wind, and so was my happiness.

-JJO

Battle of the Bands
1968

Three cheers for the only war worth fighting.

When he was in middle school, my son K.C. played in a little rock band called Sound-Sationals. (Dorky name heavily influenced by a parent who was not me.) For Christmas one year five boys were given guitars and amps—surprise!—because they had all pressured their parents for the same gift. They wanted to start a group. Santa was swayed.

Long before K.C.'s rock fame arrived, I taught him a few chords on my old 12-string Yamaha and, at age 9, he composed what became my favorite classic rock song—"I Want to Take You to Hawaii." The inspiration for this piece was his second-grade girlfriend. To escape from little brother when off to play at her house, we code named her Target Zero.

Though his sweet little rock group practiced only two hours every two weeks, K.C. practiced his guitar every day and we found that he was naturally gifted at playing songs by ear. He continued creating original tunes, even though we'd moved two states away from his original inspiration. Didn't "Layla" go on to marry someone else? So did Target Zero.

Though our middle-school boys were friends, they struggled with the usual rock-band jealousies of who sang lead, who played the most solos, who was group leader, and what clothes they should wear—the usual rock-band killers in middle-school or middle-age. Perhaps these are the reasons our boys skimped on practice time. Or perhaps it was because they all wanted to be basketball, football, and baseball stars, too.

Triumphing over this pettiness, their first, last, and pinnacle performance was at the seventh-grade science fair assembly, where they thrilled the audience with two numbers—

"Wild Thing" and "Louie, Louie." Both songs use the same chords, the same beat, and for all you and I know, "Louie, Louie" repeats "Wild Thing" lyrics. Only the Sound-Sationals know for sure.

Mosh pits were invented at this assembly when the Sound-Sationals' middle-school audience crept as close to the stage as the principal would allow. There followed much screaming for two songs and five cute tweener boys; so the Sound-Sationals enjoyed a successful public premiere *and* a sentimental farewell tour, in a "two-birds-with-one-musical-stone" kind of way.

Sound-Sationals lost the normal rock beat of their two numbers in favor of what their practice hours allowed…a slow dirge tempo like "House of the Rising Sun." Regardless, the *Papa*razzi were all over these kids. *Mama*razzi, too. Parents can't help themselves. We were proud of our babies. We were groupies. What we *weren't* were crazed modern-day Little League dads and soccer moms socking each other.

K.C., the rhythm guitarist, and two other Sationals carried their career forward into the new school year to rock their eighth-grade talent show before the ultimate breakup. Hearts were bitter. Tears were shed. Hair was pulled. When the kids told us adults to knock it off, we did.

Which brings us way, way back to the olden day Battle of the Bands…mix six rock groups made up of local high school kids; one big high school gym; a couple radio DJ's; hundreds of kids; free soda pop, potato chips, and Pizza Puffs; three hours of dancing; and, at the end of the night, a winning group. Can life get any better than this?

Two rival high schools, sometimes four, were invited to boogie down. Think of this—there was no fighting, no name calling, no politically incorrect anything, no colors displayed other than my violent navy blue and bumblebee yellow plaid slacks. In Blackfoot this scene doubled as a peace rally, it was that life-altering.

My cousin's group—The Elastic Band—traveled all the way from Utah one weekend for their Saturday in our sun. My oldest brother's group—The MydKnights—were heavy into the Battle of the Bands and won on a regular basis. They were good. Good and cool. They first wore Beach Boys-type shirts—white with big red polka dots the size of baseballs. OK, they got cooler. They graduated into black shoes, black pants, and black turtle necks—J.C. Penney meets Andy Warhol. One of the groupie moms sewed big gold lamé knight shields onto their turtle chests and her lead-singer daughter's sheath dress from the same fabric.

Then they were beyond cool. They were *groovy*. Except *groovy* wasn't a word you heard in Blackfoot, Idaho. In the late '60s, the entire '70s, definitely not the '80s, there was no *groovy* being uttered. Well, only one boy in town used this word. My boy friend (not boyfriend) used *groovy* once in a while for comedic shock. But The MydKnights *were* groovy; and I was a groupie, jealous of Linda, the lead singer among the five boy musicians.

You saw parents at the Battle of the Bands. They were the groupies, sometimes roadies. The MydKnights' trailer was built by Ron's dad. Custom paint job was by Linda's mom, who was also "seamstress for the band." Gas, so they could travel to McCammon and back was by Russ' dad (who was also my dad and gave me a lot of gas). Gas money was also hard-earned bucks from The MydKnights playing high school dance gigs all over Southeastern Idaho. Extra ampage was by Wade's dad and mom. Road treats were by Russ and Roger's moms and girlfriends. Wisecracks about the loud noise (*You call this music?)* were by Russ and Roger's dads and, well, all the dads and moms.

Lots of parental jokes at The MydKnights' expense were followed by confessions that their own parents said the same things about *their* music in the 40s and 50s. Razzing about new musical styles doesn't skip generations—jokes about rap music and various trash tunes have popped out of my mouth.

Rock band costs? Big bucks. Family time and pride in children's accomplishments? Priceless.

Eventually The MydKnights won their regional contest and went on to Twin Falls for the Idaho state Battle of the Bands. This was big time. Mom and Dad, Dean, Ken, and I were there, along with the rest of The MydKnights' roadies and groupies.

Among the bands competing was a Chicago clone group...you know, a cast of thousands with 900 of them playing brass. Very funky majestic. Our roadies and groupies were worried.

The MydKnights played their thirty minute repertoire perfectly. From "I Believe in Magic" to "Cherry Pie" to "House of the Rising Sun" and everything in between, including "Louie, Louie." Our guys were up against some stiff competition, but they never sounded better, though to my ear, compared with the Chicago-clone, our favorites seemed a little, ahem, small town. Our guys played their hearts out. People screamed. When Russ, lead guitarist, put his Yamaha up, over and behind his head, the melody screamed out of his fingers. Mayhem ensued. No one there had ever seen such a thing. I'd never seen such a thing. He rocked the house.

    I screamed loudest of all because, during my seventh-grade year, screaming was my job. And as a tweener groupie—for real, for the first time—I finally realized I didn't need Davy Jones, Bobby Sherman, Paul McCartney, *or* pretty Ricky Nelson. I had The MydKnights. And I had an *in*.

    There with my groupies in be-bop heaven, a tall stranger, a lanky Twin Falls High School boy asked me to dance. Mom looked shocked. I *was* shocked, but played it as cool as a MydKnight. Didn't he know I was in seventh-grade? Didn't he know this was the dress I wore my afternoon junior high school Valentine's Dance, where it took the boys long enough, duh, to ask me to dance? Didn't he notice that these white shoes made me look like Minnie Mouse but they were the only thing that sorta matched this red dress? Didn't he know there was Clearasil at the drugstore for all his zits? Well, anyway, this was thrilling!

    Put a Smiley-Face sticker on this day.

    I went. I danced. And when the Chicago-clones got too groovy and the beat was undanceable, we all stopped to listen. Lanky Boy put his arm around my waist. I was uncomfortable with that move. I shifted from foot to foot, trying to clue him in that I wasn't a girl to let just any strange boy's arm dangle around her waist at every Battle of the Bands. He didn't get my subtle signals.

    When Chicago-clone finished playing, I thanked spotted Lanky Boy and went back to my own crowd. Kenny, my fourth-grade baby brother, blurted out to my folks, "Julie danced with that boy and...he was *hugging* her when they stopped dancing."

    "Oh, he was *not*. Jist shut up." Only my vastly superior maturity kept me from slugging him...as he stood right next to my parents. He was lucky we were in public when he tattled. I danced the rest of the night with groupie boy children who were not my brothers. (Aside: You may be happy to know that Ken arrived alive to enjoy today, and I don't say *shut up* to him anymore. He's a distinguished professor, a *Dr.,* who doesn't tattle any longer. For years he entertained crowds playing guitar and mandolin in a top-notch bluegrass band. Oh, and when I became a mom, in my house I declared s*hut up* to be a swear word.)

At the end of the night we had rock 'n' rolled through all eight bands and it was time for the big announcement. I was sure the Chicago-clones were going to win. They were too, for when they were announced in second place and went onstage to collect their $500 prize money, they were much less thrilled than I was at Lanky Boy's dance invitation.

"And now for the winners. Our judges think the winning band has a great sound. They're all excellent musicians, so skilled and accomplished at their craft. When this group competes in the national Battle of the Bands in Atlantic City, New Jersey, later this year, Idaho will give the rest of the country a run for their money! What set this band apart from all the other groups was their wide range of songs. They played a variety of music, from slow ballads to classic rock, tunes fun to listen to and fun to dance to, and that the crowd tonight certainly enjoyed. Your 1968 Idaho Battle of the Bands champions are.....The MydKnights!"

Wild applause! Much screaming, many tears, smiles all around, big trophy, waving, autographs, cameras, paparazzi and mamarazzi. You'd think all of us MydKnight groupies could show a little dignity with our win. But no, it was all as it should have been.

K.C. and The Sound-Sationals would have loved it.

Nationally, The MydKnights placed in the Top Ten in this United States of America. We had a hard time believing the dream was reality. They cut a demo tape and would have gone on to sell something if the *papa*razzi and *mama*razzi had had any gas money left over to help them out, and had thought of themselves as "record producers" as well as "farmers." But there's only so much you can sacrifice to a chancy rock music career in a small farm community when the mortgage payment still sings loud and strong and the old tractor has to be fixed with baling wire. And that was when gas was 35¢ per gallon instead of $35 per gallon.

The choices between good, better, best—private battles, cool conflicts—never end.

The MydKnights continued to play southeastern Idaho before some of our idols went off to college or missions for our church. My brother's best friend, Wade, who played MydKnight organ, was a newlywed expecting his first baby when he was killed in a tragic motorcycle accident. So, new band members came and went. Gradually, as our stars grew into their 20s, got married, and settled down, infant children filled MydKnight lives and rock music evolved into rocking lullabies.

It was all as it should have been—skirmishes worth fighting.

After the glory days, when Linda married and moved to Nevada, I begged Russ to let me replace her as lead singer. He resisted, for what reason I never knew. Maybe it was my voice. And little siblings can cramp your style.

Then I was off to college and he was relieved from sisterly petitions. One glorious summer just before The MydKnights broke up forever, my two girl cousins from Seattle were in town visiting grandma, passing through, packed up and ready for our sophomore year at college. Russ let us come up on stage, shake the tambourines, and sing backup. The "great pretenders" had a blast. The three of us were at the same microphone, performing our hearts out. We were beyond cool. Russ told us after the night was over that our mic was turned down as low as they could possibly crank it.

The past few years, (decades, I suppose) when I go home to visit and ask Russ to play "Cherry Pie," he says, "I don't think I can remember the words," and doesn't even bother going upstairs to get his acoustic guitar. I sigh and wish once more that I had been in Linda's lamé dress.

When did our playing stop?

Even now, when I hear my favorite golden oldies, I can't help saying, *The MydKnights used to play that song.* The good news is that Russ just purchased his dream guitar, so maybe the music will come back to him.

Between the three of us, brothers and sister, surely all the words can be remembered.

I sing along to something trapped inside me. I like to say *wah-wah pedal* and *whammy bar* and wish to use one. I feel the awkward arms of a spotted boy around my waist. I start the same old white-girl shuffle on the dance floor. My lips automatically curve up into a smile. My body can't resist the pull of the music, the battle of the bands, on a hot summer night. This is my kind of time warp.

It's a battle—a very sweet battle.

You can't step into the same river twice.
-Heraclitus

**Whoa Back and Cowboy Up!
or
Synchronize Your Watches**
1995

    I had a hard time getting out of bed this morning. It felt like I'd driven the Indy 500 overnight—or been driven over by the Indy 500.
    Maybe it's because of my dream. I always have interesting dreams and I remember them. In last night's dream, Tim from "Home Improvement" (this was a definite step up from my tornado nightmare and the spinach-pulling-out-all-my-teeth dream) and I were doing something on stage together. It must have been thrilling. I was blindfolded.
    Maybe it's dreams. Maybe it's because of how my evenings go. Take last night for example...

    Mark has karate at 3:40. Steve takes him to the dojo and does a few errands while he's waiting for Mark to finish. I prepare dinner while they're gone.
    Erin studies first and then hangs out at Xio's house.
    Nick has a class meeting after school and then gets a haircut. He drives home just in time so that when K.C. calls from cross-country practice at his middle school needing a ride home in the rain, I have a vehicle here.
    Steve retrieves Mark at 4:30.
    Nick is kind enough to go get K.C. at 4:35.
    Steve and Mark and Nick and K.C. all magically arrive home at 5:00.

Erin thinks she must take the two little girls she's babysitting to their swim practice in Bellevue tonight. We must leave at 5:10 to do this. She gets home from Xio's at 5:07. Just before she gets home, Little Girls' mother calls and tells me we don't need to take her daughters to Bellevue tonight. Good.

Since we are all together now and dinner just happens to be ready, we sit down and—miracle of miracles!—dine together as a family, something social scientists and spiritual leaders tell us is vital for the world's survival. We believe this. It is a joyous occasion. I have prepared grade-school beans on Erin's behalf; her favorite green beans from the can, the kind that lunch ladies just open and heat. For some strange reason, picky eater that she's become, Erin loves grade-school beans. Some days I'm a lunch lady.

Steve, Nick, Erin, and K.C. have Youth Standards Night tonight at the church. Since Erin has dance rehearsal tonight for an upcoming recital, she will miss this special youth meeting. The original plan was for Erin and me to take her two Little Girls to Bellevue early, go back to Fabricland for a zipper, then on to dance.

Suddenly, plans have changed. Instead of staying at rehearsal tonight, I must turn right around, a 25 mile round trip, and get the van back for Steve. We needed the van to drive the girls around. Steve now needs the van to carpool kids to Standards Night since he is the Young Men's President. Erin and I can take the truck instead.

Despite what mother of Little Girls said, she calls a second time and suddenly plans change again! Whoa back! Erin and I deliver Little Girls in the van to Bellevue for swim team practice. The zipper is purchased. At 6:20 I drop off Erin at ballet and at 6:22 I'm on I-90 as originally planned, speeding eastbound back to Issaquah.

At 6:29, Steve, Nick, and K.C. leave home to meet the other teens and adults at Klahanie Information Center to carpool to Bellevue. The three of them are forced to cram into the little truck to drive to the Info Center.

At 6:35, I meet Steve, Nick and K.C. at the Info Center. We switch vehicles. They, plus more, jump into the van. I crawl into the truck.

At 6:37, I'm on my way home to 10-year-old Mark, who is Home Alone. Steve is on his way with the van full of youth to their special meeting.

At 6:40, I am home with Mark. We read the Seattle Times, do homework, and watch the Mariners whip the Cleveland Indians.

At 8:00, Steve slips out of the Youth Standards meeting in Bellevue and picks up Erin at ballet, drives back with her to finish their meeting, and then loads up his van full of kids for the ride home at 8:39, when he drops off four extra teens at their doorsteps.

At 9:00, everyone who belongs at my house is finally, thankfully, back home and getting ready for bed. Where are Little Girls? I have no idea. I'm too tired to care. I'm hoping their daddy did indeed pick them up from swim practice.

Slow down.

One question, you ask. Why are *you* driving the Little Girls Erin baby-sits to Bellevue for swim-team practice when you are already so busy with your own family?

Simple reason. The mother of the swimming Little Girls has never learned how to drive! Mother of Little Girls is afraid to drive. She pays other people to drive her children around and to drive her around. Her husband allegedly picks his girls up on his way home from work in Bellevue later on in the evening. At least, that's what we're told. Little Girls show up again at our house every day after school, so maybe it is so.

One of my grandmas never learned how to drive. She didn't need to in the olden days. When Grandma rode with us we always let her ride shotgun, out of respect and love. (For Grandma, not the shotgun position. And she didn't even know to call *shotgun*.) Once in awhile I got to drive with Grandma by my side. In Idaho we got our driver's licenses at 14! Fourteen! We drove tractors, don't ya know. I could feel Grandma tense up and quietly lean back in her seat if I was driving too fast. Out of the corner of my eye, I watched her press her right foot down hard on the car floor in a futile attempt to control this juvenile's speed. Prrresss...so I'd speed up a fraction, with my eyes on the road, my hands at 10 and 2. Grandma never verbally expressed her passenger fears. Her body language did all the talking.

Mother of swimming Little Girls, why are you afraid to drive? You ride in cars. Are you afraid to drive because you know that if you drive you will have evenings like the ones I have almost every night?

Whoa, I say to you, *Cowboy Up*! I am busy and so is everyone else. You shouldn't depend on us to drive your busy children around. Cowboy up, my sister.

This driving of Little Girls is an act of service as well as a little job for Erin. We're going that way, we can drive them, even though, like tonight, it is inconvenient. We don't love Little Girls or their mother like we loved Grandma. This will not last.

We all took turns driving Grandma for forty years. It was a great way to hang out with Grandma and get her to tell stories of plow horses; of how Grandpa courted her with hollyhocks when they were sixteen and freshly spunky; of how she saved her own little children every summer from drowning in the irrigation ditch next to her clothesline. We were happy to chauffeur Grandma.

I learned to whoa down and listen, but long after I was fourteen.

Mother of Little Girls, you who are afraid to get a driver's license and chauffeur your own kids, you are missing out on some quiet time alone when you can listen to your children and hear what's on their minds. You can watch them out of the corner of your eyes to see if there is happiness in their faces. Cowboy up, my sister. It is good to trap them in cars. Turn off the radio, ban personal CD players, hold on tight to the tidbits they toss your way. Cherish tidbits. Learn to juggle thoughts and feelings with them the way you juggle schedules. Whoa back. Spend a quantity of time driving your own kids around and quality time will happen.

That is why I can have evenings like the one I just described and survive them, even thrive on them.

I'm so glad Grandma never learned to drive.

I wish my children had never learned to drive.

Wove, Twue Wove
1972

I will now do an Interpretive Rendering for you. The topic is *wove*. Using the finest, most lyrical, most devastating, dramatic, most *yearning* poetry—which became love songs played in the same three chords on my little brown Yamaha guitar—I will *emote* the deep passions of a 16-year-old high school junior. I will *expose* the depths of my *wove, twue wove.*

You will recognize the depths. Perhaps you are in the throes of it right now. But just because you will recognize the depths vividly doesn't mean you can remember clearly how pathetic one can become when embracing *wove* or wallowing in its depths. I may be exposing your patheticism at the same moment I expose my *wove.* Forgive me.

Wove. This stuff happens. My first *twue wove* smoldered in the direction of an *older* man on his way to med school. Actually my first *twue wove* was more like a brush fire—fast and stinky. Flames, short-lived in the summer of '72, are long remembered, as first *woves* always are. Rest assured that my 1972 self has granted me permission to make public these sacred expressions of hunka-hunka burnin' *wove.*

Herein, will I Render Interpretations of my song-poems, and will follow each poem with the modern mature Accurate Elucidation (a large, college-type word meaning 'explanation' or 'to make clear.') which was totally obscured by Coke-bottle-bottom rosy-colored glasses way back then.

Hindsight may be 20/20, but it's not always rosy.

The bloom long, long gone off your first *wove, twue wove* may be trying to sprout its wild blossom upon your heart once again with a new *wove* like the white-blossomed morning glory weed tries to strangle the tomato plants in your vegetable garden. And so, there is great value in Interpretive Renderings with Accurate Elucidations. The danger of Interpretive Renderings *without* Accurate Elucidations is what happens when the morning glory never gets yanked out by its roots and your tomatoes, in fact, get strangled. Then you must make your BLT without the T, and there just ain't the same flavor or quality in a BL.

First Selection–
(Sung to the guitar chords of G-C-F)

Us
Maybe it's that kind of day,
Or maybe it's just your special way.
All I know is when I see you
I'm happy, so happy, inside.

When I first met you,
I knew I could never forget you,
And I wanted you never to forget me.
Please, let me be your friend.

When it happened—
You and me became...us,
I knew I could live as I had never lived before.

Now I'm happy,
As I've never been happy before.
Now I can care and now I can love
As I've never cared and loved before.
What's more, I really love you.

Maybe it's that kind of day,
But I think it's your special way,
All I know is now I'm happy, so happy, inside.
Please, let me be your friend, forever.

First Elucidation–
    He was seven years older than me, a college graduate of 24. Compared with the juvenile peasant high school boys I knew

he was an Adonis. Since I was just beginning to get it, that I could never claim in marriage Bobby Sherman, Shaun Cassidy, Michael Landon, Pernell Roberts, or, especially, our favorite Monkee, Davy Jones, (even if I rode horses really well) I knew that Adam (a made-up name of great symbolism in a syncopated nod to both the Bible and the Ponderosa) was my first and only *wove, twue wove.*

What I know now is that even though my high school peasant boys were not Adonises, they were my buds; and buds are more valuable by a long shot than false gods and idols, even if they are Adams, Bobbys or Monkees.

The other truth I'm exposing now is that I was very happy before I met Adam, but my adolescent self didn't want to acknowledge it. That would have made my mother's notions about me correct, and there was no way I was going to acknowledge *that.*

Second Selcction–
(Sung to the guitar chords of C-F-G)

Wait For Me

You say I'm too young for you.
May I ask, then what can I do?
Could you wait for me to grow up, please?
Would you wait for me to grow up? Please do.

Do years make the difference to you?
Is it time that makes a difference, too?
My mind has grown, my thoughts have flown
Each day that I've known you.
Could you wait for me to grow up, please?
Would you wait for me to grow up? Please do.

Each night I kneel and pray, and ask the Lord
For one more day,
To understand, to make a stand, to prove
Myself to you.
Could you wait for me to grow up, please?
Would you wait for me to grow up? Please do.

I understand that you are a man

With lots of things to do.
But you are a man who could understand
The feeling I have for you.
Could you wait for me to grow up, please?
Would you wait for me to grow up?
Please...I want you to.

Second Elucidation–
When, as an eighth-grader, I used to pore over my oldest brother Russ' high school yearbook and the yearbooks of neighboring towns, admiring all the older men in the annuals of time, little did I know that in just six short years, I would actually be dancing to Chicago's *Color My World* in the arms of my second favorite older local dreamboat.

I confess that I did not actually pray to prove myself to Adam. My lyrics lie. Nor did I pray for some kind of time warp that would allow me to skip over the next seven years of my life and become 24 overnight, although at the time it would have seemed a blessed phenomenon.

Yep, my thoughts flew. Adam taught me how to kiss. We fogged up his Firebird windows a little bit one night after our ninth date. Kissing up some window steam was as far as we ever went. Boy, am I glad. You already know why. You know where we're headed.

My mind grew and my thoughts flew, all right. One romantic night in the basement of his parents' house, Adam wove a delicate ring of blue and white Indian beads and slipped it on my ring finger, asking me if I'd live with him if he wasn't married upon his graduation from med school. As my lips parted softly, dewily, the naked light bulb dangling from the asbestos ceiling cast sparkling diamondy reflections on my gently *yearning* lips, my eyes glazed over with the excruciations of *twue wove* and I murmured 'yes', all the while knowing that we would never do that; good Mormon girls and boys who are living the wise moral principles of their religion don't live with their *woves* out of wedlock. They get married. They save the sacred for after marriage. Nevertheless, I was shocked, thrilled, and flattered—all the while knowing in my heart of hearts that he didn't mean it at all. And neither did I.

Truthfully, I pictured a diamond on that ring finger to replace the blue and white beads. In a little misty dream bubble above my head I saw myself cooking up a big batch of No Bakes for my *twue* husband who had had a rough day passing medical exams. Sadly (or not) I lost my blue and white ring months later at my high school graduation party, while playing Red Rover with my girlfriends and buds. The dream bubble burst.

Third Selection–
(Sung to the guitar chords of F-G-C)

I Know You Better Than You Think

Sometimes you make me laugh.
Sometimes you make me cry.
But isn't that what it's all about?
Learning the how and why.

So don't tell me you can't ever be my love.
Don't tell me you can't ever love.
For I've seen you pick a flower and
Hold it gently in your hand.
Then softly give your newfound life to me.

Words control one, I know.
It's words that make a feeling slow.
But I've seen that look in your eye, my love,
Even if you've never told me so.

So don't tell me you can't ever be that way.
Don't tell me you can't share your love.
For I've seen you take the trembling hand
Of a child in the dark,
And kindly share the light of your love.

You tell me not to try and look
Too deep inside your soul.
Keep the door shut tight and the darkness is your own.
But I get a certain feeling that
That's not really true.
Can I find the key and then we'll really know?

So don't tell me you can't ever care, my love.
Don't tell me you can't be that way.
For I've seen you take the pain and fears

> Of my own soul
> And with your love you've pushed the hurt away.
>
> So don't tell me you can't ever care.
> Don't tell me you don't want to try.
> For I've seen you give yourself
> In your own special way.
> And, that is the way of love, after all.

Third Elucidation–

Adam knew he could never be my *twue wove* (even though he liked kissing me an awful lot) because he knew he was off to med school after our *torrid* summer romance. The look in his eye was not *Wove with a capital W*, it was Wust with a capital L. I like to believe there was a little love mixed in, but the guy had a hard time remembering my name over three summer months. Granted, he could never remember anyone's name, (a sign of selfishness and a distracted mind) but he steamed up windows with me, for Pete's sake. I wish I'd kept my lips to myself and my windows transparent.

The trembling child's hand in the dark? Mine, of course. Well, OK, Adam had some other little toddler type friends and some nieces. One night we were invited to dinner at his former college roommate's house and Adam wanted desperately for me *not* to tell them I was still in high school. After putting her toddler to bed, the roommate's wife and I were in the kitchen cooking green beans while the men were in the living room chewing over the good old days of '71. When she asked me what I was doing with my life, I cleverly told her I was still a student, skillfully not divulging which type. Pursuing the conversation, she asked where I went to college. Honestly, I would kiss the guy, but I was *not* going to lie about my grade in school for him. So I revealed the shocking truth. She was good enough not to gasp, scream, or laugh out loud and send Adam spiraling down into apoplectic shock—something he hadn't studied yet and so couldn't cure himself of at a dinner party. But when supper was over and we were settled into his Firebird for the drive home, he mentioned something about my spilling the beans and he didn't mean at the table. Do the math—he was SEVEN years old and playing cops and robbers when I was being squeezed out of my mother's BIRTH CANAL.

I know this now, but was too young to know it then: Adam didn't want me to look deep inside his soul because I'd see: 1.) Lust, but we've already covered that topic. 2.) He was scared about going off to med school and wanted to remain a manly man in my eyes. 3.) He didn't want to be responsible for sharing anything of deep significance with me, a peasant, a little summer *wove*. 4) I'd discover that when he grew up and made some money from doctoring, his favorite pastime would be to go off and kill lots of exotic animals to plaster all over every wall he owned.

When Adonises are telling you they can't really love or care about you the way you want them to, and they can't let you into their thoughts and hearts, you better believe them and stop wishing it was so. Thus the popular saying: "he's just not that into you." Or, as my timeless saying goes: "Where the *wust* is, there will the heartless be, also." Which sounds like a proverb from the Bible, or something just as truthful. Even s*inging* those wishes to the same three chords on your Yamaha guitar will not make it so, either.

Forrest Gump's mama was right—stupid is as stupid does—and Forrest was smart enough to listen. My mama tried to tell me—naive is as naive does. Forrest was lots smarter than me.

Fourth Selection –
(Sung to the guitar chords of C-F-G. In the stylings of The Carpenters meet The Kinks.)

Quickly Comes The Sunset

Quickly comes the sunset
Even though we need the day.
Yes, I mind you going.
I always knew it had to be that way.

I let my thoughts lie vacant
As I watch the clouds roll by.
But in my mind I wonder
And ask the question...why?

Why do bees sting?
Why do birds sing?

Why does rain fall?
Why do I have to care at all?

You are you, I am me.
We are guided by our visions
Perfect as they may be.

Why do bees sting?
Why do birds sing?
Why does rain fall?
Why do I have to care at all?

Friends are friends.
That's what you said.
And now your words
Are running through my head.

And I still mind you going.
I knew it would turn out this way.
But I still mind you going.
I'll be here when you come back someday.

Fourth Elucidation–

    Shoulda—seen that my vision about *wove* was way shortsighted, and way *imperfect,* not *perfect* as my lyrics would lull you into thinking. Plus, I was way short-changing myself, which is not unlike short sheeting your own bed. A cruel joke on yourself.

    Coulda—seen the above, wearing my contact lenses (not the eyeglasses from my seventh-grade Mrs. Allen period) with some extra-long-range vision into the future decade and beyond. If you're clever, you discover one day that high school isn't your total world forever—it's the size of a BB among all the bigger roly-poly things in the circle of life.

    Woulda—been lots happier admitting to my heart that Adam was just a summer *wove,* as temporary as the high school teachers I tolerated, as imperfect as the high school boys I slighted. Big difference: My teachers cared about enriching me and my buds cared about being good friends to me.

Fifth Selection–
(a Jethro Tull kind of dirge sung to the chords of G-F-C. I'm too busy being in morose *wove* to learn new chords.)

Sad

Thoughts go by.
Just inside.
Nothing's real.
Nothing comes.
I am here.
My heart is here.
As I wait
Nothing comes.
Why do I still care?
You are gone.
Who knows where.
You said goodbye
And I cried.
You said goodbye
And I died inside.
I am here.
My heart's still here.
And I wait.
Nothing comes.

Fifth Elucidation–

While the thoughts of Adam were stagnating and fermenting and moldering like a Halloween mummy all up inside my *yearning* nostrils, I was missing out on a lot of truly important ponderings, lots more laughter and fun with my friends, lots more appreciation for my senior year of high school, and lots of anticipation for my own college experience.

Another Big Plus would have been: I wouldn't have forgotten to do my mythology project in my college prep English class. I'm sorry, Mrs. Gardner. I woke up remembering it was deadline morning. I woke up that deadline morning in a panic. I'm sorry for the miserable little paper doll I grabbed off of my closet shelf. I'm sorry for the miserable makeover I gave her to try to make her become Pandora. I'm sorry for Scotch-taping her to a tinfoil covered Cream of Wheat box. I'm sorry I pretended to bring in Pandora with her box. I'm sorry I had to call it good. It wasn't. Let's just blame it on Adam the Adonis. I wish I could have covered him up in a tinfoil casket, brought him to your classroom and set him on the shelf wearing a paper headstone that read: "Here lies Adonis. Killed in action by green beans and a Yamaha guitar." Now that's the stuff mythology is made of. Mrs. Gardner, you will be glad to know that while I muffed an important assignment because of him, I was no longer fogging up any windows with him.

Sixth Selection–
(Big chord change here! I learned 3 new ones. Take note! Dm-C-Emaj7-Am-E-A)

Hope Song

You hide your feelings well.
You hide your feelings
But I think I can tell.
Don't deny the love you have for me.
Don't deny the love that could be ours.

You want me to forget you
And what we had.
All the things we felt
And the good things shared.
Well, it's been some time
Since I saw you last.
But how can you expect me
to forget the past?

Yes, I know there are many things
Which cannot be.
I will wait until our union
You can see.
Let it be.
Let it come naturally.
Don't (some scribble I can't read anymore)
Eternally.

Sixth Elucidation–
    A-wishin' and a-hopin' and a-singin' still won't make the *wove* dream come *twue*. The "some time" since I had seen him last was three and a half months. Adam came home for Christmas break, we had one date, and we kissed two more times. He couldn't see our "union" which, translated, meant he was supposed to be my boyfriend again. But, rats, my worst fears were true—he was blinded by too many college coeds and shocking exams up north in Seattle.
    Whatever I scribbled in my original song-poem notebook between "Don't" and "Eternally" *should* have been: "Don't expect me to drool over you, now or eternally." I know that's not what I wrote. It was something else sappy and false.

Seventh Selection–
(Sung to the same tired old chords of C-F-G-Fm7-C7-Am. In the stylings of The Carpenters meet Iron Butterfly. Long and drawn out like *In-A-Gadda-Da-Vida Why Do Birds Suddenly Appear*.)

                Time Gone

                See the leaves fall,
        Like the tears I shed for you.
          Where is the man I knew?

           Gone, gone, gone, gone.
Like the summer days, when we used to play.
            Gone, gone, gone now
              To the autumn sky.

                See the snow fall.
      Silently, softly, you used to call.
    Where there was love, there's nothing at all.

           Gone, gone, gone, gone.
       Autumn leaves soon will go.
         Gone, gone, gone, now.
           To the winter day.

              Hear the birds sing.
  Cold winter day has now turned to spring.
         Gone is the coldness you

Left for me in my heart.

Gone, gone, gone, gone.
The sparkling snow in the meadow.
Gone, gone, gone now
To the spring day.

April showers, see the flowers,
See how quickly time passes by.

Gone, gone, gone, gone,
Gone is the coldness I felt
For you in my heart.
Gone, gone, gone, gone.
My feelings have changed as the seasons
That pass through my life.
Gone, gone, gone now
To a new day.

Seventh Elucidation–
We see a glimmer of hope here! I am slowly coming back to my senses. Scoop up all those fallen autumn leaves, scrape them into a big pile, jump in them a whole bunch, and then burn them up. Ashes to ashes, dust to dust, our tender union was all a bust. I was beginning to forgive him for dumping me and being a jerk, although I still couldn't say to myself: He was a jerk who used you for the summer then dumped you.

Our last date, Christmas 1973, after returning home from my freshman semester at college...when what to my wondering eyes had appeared but a whole campus full of Adonises! Too cool. Adam never told me there were so many glorious fish in the univer-Sea-ty! When I saw him again that Christmas I released him back into the wild without a hook in his mouth, recognizing our experience for what it was—a teensy bit real, a whole lot counterfeit.

There is a happy ending. After New Year's 1974 I went back to BYU, had a great scholastic experience, met my real *Wove Twue Wove*, got married, had four kids, have some beautiful grandkids, and in 2009 will have been married for 33 years full of steamy windows.

So go and give this essay to your own kids, or your grandkids, if any of them are having fits of *wove* or *wust*. Or give it to yourself. And if you don't *get* it, you must go back and *sing* all my *yearning* songs over and over and over again until you do get it.

While you do that, I will go and give my *Wove, Twue Wove* a big old juicy kiss before I sit him down and sing him my best new Wove songs sung to the guitar chords of C-F-G.

One man's punishment is another man's party.

One Blind Mouse

Perhaps like a mouse you are mesmerized.
Closing in on cheese,
but sensing danger.
Not knowing how to collect your prize
without becoming captive.

Snap and clutch,
steel, wood, contraption.
Dangerous.
Ridiculous.
Un-sprung.
Never set.
False torture.
Whimsy.

Our differences ensnare us.
Our similarities free us.
Our actions break us.
Our dreams heal us.
Our relationship puzzles us.

Someone should invent a better one.

It's like going for the bait,
and collecting a sliver
instead of springing the trap.

Slivers are only a part of our collection.

-Julie J. Oliver
1972

Everything I Know I Learned In a Crab Pot
2001

If you've got the guts to move to an island as a full-time resident, you have the right to be called an "islander" from the moment your big yellow Ryder truck rolls off the ferry and you snap your first toilet paper roll in place. Don't let the arrogance of the "old-timers" fool you. They'll still call you a tourist even after you've been on the island for twenty years.

You *must* start learning the ways of the island before you get there. Like how not to get stranded in the standby ferry line. There is nothing sadder than missing the ferry you need by just one little red Hyundai. When you're at Arby's scarfing down the five-for-$5 deal in the big city and that quiet little intuition pokes you in the gut, you should listen. Grab those curly fries, your fifty paper thimbles full of Arby's Sauce, and head for the docks. You can always eat, drink, and potty on the ferry.

It is a sad, sad day when the 5:05 pulls out and leaves you behind as the first car in line for the 8:35. Knowing the last ferry takes three hours rather than one because it stops at all the islands and yours is the last island in the archipelago, your life flashes before your eyes as the orange-vested ferry worker leans on the hood of your car, smiles, and says, "That's it for the five. Relax and enjoy the view."

We're islanders who have to go off island three times a month. We've enjoyed the view often. Trust me: If you're unprepared at the mainland docks for the three-hour wait until the last ferry arrives, you know you're doomed to memorizing this week's Thrifty Nickel to pass the time. That's a lot of Nickel.

Let me help you come prepared for a lifetime, or just a visit to an island.

Preparedness means bringing a loaf of bread. You can make friends with the seagulls and crows and your neighbors in line. See how many birds you can get to land on your car before one of them drops a souvenir on your bumper or your shoulder. Some old-timer might show you that bird poop is taking the fender off his car faster than the rust is. Some tourist will clutch her children close to her bosom in fright. Dogs will point. Crows think this is funny and laugh at all of it.

Preparedness is packing Power Bars, Costco mixed nuts, Fruit-by-the Yard, and a big jug of water in your trunk. Stupefying boredom is an option, but a mystery novel, or a deck of cards and a Yahtzee game to share with your fellow riders is more fun. A blanket and pillow are handy too, if you're a tired, boring person. Forget the empty mayo jars—there are bathrooms at the landing and on the ferries.

As a new islander it gradually dawns on you that your household water pressure drizzles out of your tap at the general pace of the island. This is simply a reminder that life is to be savored here. Also that you mustn't drive like you're still 16 years old. You must pretend to drive like you're a relaxed adult familiar with island life.

There are no stoplights here, just twelve stop signs. Traffic flow sometimes follows the state driving code, sometimes not. One never honks on the island. Tailgating is abhorred. You must look the other driver in the eyes and wave, or everyone absolutely knows you're a tourist, except other tourists. Don't even think of passing anyone, even if Farmer John and Fisherman Bob create a blockade on the only street out of town to chat about the San Juan County Fair 4-H rules. You *always* stop for deer, quail, foxes, raccoons, and gawkers peering into art galleries from the middle of the town's six official pedestrian crossings. Canada geese and town dogs know they don't have the right of way, but will take advantage of you if you let them. Swing wide for joggers, bicyclists, rental mopeds, and scoot-cars.

You learn to spot a tourist right away. Their clothes match. They don't have big gray beards to keep the chin warm. Their heads swivel constantly looking at stuff. They go early to create a line for movies at the Palace Theater where, for Harry Potter and hobbit films, a big crowd is twelve people. They're either pale white all over, ethnic colors all over, or tan all over—no fisherman or farmer tans peeking out of long johns. They eat ice cream cones on the streets. They wear sunglasses and smiles. And the most obvious sign—they laugh loudly in new vacation T-shirts.

On Spring Street, where the pier ends and the water rules with great force, you learn quickly that "deadheads" are not Jerry Garcia fans. Fast, noisy Jet Skis are absolutely outlawed, as are bullet bikes on land. You observe the rhythm of the tides and how beautiful and dangerous they can be. You take an extra jacket to the beach because it's always cooler near the water. A cotton ball comes in handy and is easy to carry and pull apart to stuff in your ears in a cold summer breeze. Earmuffs are embarrassing in July.

If you love seafood, you learn how to eat from the ocean. There are ocean secrets for gathering crabs, oysters, clams, and mussels just as there are river secrets to lure rainbow trout from an Idaho stream. I didn't know these exotic ocean fishing methods as a teenager pulling Brook trout from Cherry Creek. It's a light-bulb island moment when you discover that copper rockfish are used as bait, not your entrée. They are rich, buttery and delicious though, and I'm not too proud to eat bait.

Each of us will always have a lot to learn, even on a small island, so it's a wonderful thing to receive shared secrets from old-timers. (Thanks, Jerry, for cluing us in to Lingcod bait. See above.)

Sometimes you just can't, or won't, learn from others' mistakes. Sometimes it's just plain impossible to learn vicariously—you have to live your own lessons. Here are some tips from me to you, some of which are hard-learned. If you're wise, they will help feed you when you are famished.

1. Be creative. Positioning bait in the trap is important. You don't want your crabs to just gather around outside and snack through to the inside of your pot like it's some cocktail party. Crabs are crazy for certain kinds of bait, the stinkier the better. You'd think fish heads from the bay would be the exclusive meal, but no-o-o...Western Family skinless smoked hot dogs, Friskies chicken and liver cat food dinners, and Beach Cliff Sardines in Mustard Sauce work nicely. But your leftovers from the fridge, good stuff like rotten chicken thighs and moldy Swiss cheese will draw the biggest crowd.

Sometimes the surprisingly subtle reaps the greatest reward.

2. **Be aware.** Crab pots don't look like teapots or crockpots; they are big square, open-wire traps. Drop your pots on the incoming tide and you'll be more successful. Don't drop your pots in strong currents. And for Pete's sake, don't drop them when harbor seals are spying on you. Both will steal everything that's dear to you.

Appreciate beauty, but don't be naïve.

3. **Be safe.** Crabbing can cause your life to flash before your eyes, especially if you go out in a little red canoe to be At One With Nature. Always watch the wind, the waves, and the weather. Don't dawdle in front of the ferry, big sailboats, or an outboard motor captain waving beer cans while traveling 40 knots per second with his back to you, pontificating into the face of his equally dazed first mate. Keep an eye out for "deadheads" (big free-floating logs) and large rocks that will rip your underside open and spill your life into the sea.

Trust the goodness of your environment, but think ahead.

4. **Be selective.** How do you tell boy crabs from girl crabs? And why would you want to? How do you tell if they're mature? Just like in the landlubber world—their underbellies look different. Check out the shell markings: males are the "Washington Monument" and females are the "Little House on the Prairie." Why do you need to know this? It's illegal to collect "houses," unlike playing Monopoly. Drop any "houses" you collect back into the ocean neighborhood to keep the beloved crab population growing. The "monument," however, is legal to eat, so you must have in your possession a little yellow crab ruler. Keep it handy, measure, and then fling into your boat only those males with "monument" markings bigger than five inches. In this case, size matters.

Choose quality. Don't settle for something just to be reeling in a catch.

5. **Be sensitive.** I never knew crabs could talk to

each other. They're like two little keyboards chattering wildly, scuttling around in your sink, jabbering instant messengers. Acknowledge this life. Look at them. Listen up.
Act appropriately.

6. Be wise. You can choose the choice, but not the consequences. Use a very large cooking pot to boil your fresh catch. Bring your water to a rolling boil, then drop your crabs in quickly. There's nothing sadder than apologetically poking the last crab into a pot of boiling water already stuffed with crabs. The last crab in will backstroke out of the pot off the shells of his fellow…er, dinner mates. (See #5 Be Sensitive and #7 Be Prepared). There *can* be too much of a good thing. A small pot will stifle your output.
Execute a healthy plan without hesitation.

7. Be prepared. Watch your fingers because crabs really can pinch. To the bone. Once they're cooked, continue your dinner prep by cleaning out the crab innards at the sink, NOT at the table, or your appetite will drift away like a helium balloon at the state fair. Have enough shell crackers and nut pickers for each person. When you're on the quest for a large piece of crabmeat, it's a bummer having to share crackers and pickers. When you sit down to eat, allow plenty of time to pick out all the meat, so you're not crunching on tiny bits of shell.
Patience is the key to getting the most out of the heart of the matter.

8. Be kind. Don't let dogs or sons tease the captive crustaceans. And don't use crabs to tease your dogs or your children. Big, loud-woofing intimidator dogs and tall teenage boys may be afraid of little red crustaceans. However, the classic fear of the unknown can be overcome with gradual exposure. Respect heart.
Empathize with the large and the small. You never know when you'll be which.

To quote a favorite old-timer, Dr. Seuss: *Oh, the places you'll go!*
Oh, the new adventures you have waiting for you on an island. If you're a crustatarian you can dine on sumptuous

seafood. If you're a vegetarian, then you can relish the side salad. And if you're a slow learner, you just keep eating the bait.

I remind you of the one thing we should all know by now, islander or not: There comes a time in your life when you have to fish or cut bait.

Got guts? Then you've got island and you've got crab.

I've Been 16 for 34 Years - BoomerTweener

**"Oh The Weather Outside Is Frightful"
or
The Mighty Wind of 2006
And Why This Christmas Card Is Late**

Dec. 13 – Newscasters predict storm of the century. Julie fills up all pitchers and camp jugs with water just before Steve calls to remind her to fill pitchers and jugs with water. Both fill up gas tanks without thinking there might be trouble in paradise.

Dec. 14 – 6:33 p.m. – Steve, Mark, and Julie on couch as TV and lights go out. We sit stupefied, wondering if Mythbusters will find rockets strong enough to propel Dummy Annie around top bar of swing set and dispel myth that you can swing hard enough to send yourself around top bar of swingset. Get out lots of candles. Glad we have wood-burning stove. Early darkness makes us more tired than usual. Go to bed at 9 p.m. Steve snores. Julie listens to big branches crashing down in big wind gusts. Steve and Julie snort bolt upright out of sleep as huge tree near house snaps and crackles to the ground. Steve goes downstairs to sleep.

Dec. 15 – Wake up stupefied. Power still out. Phone no worky. Hope kids are OK. Hear helicopters overhead. Bummed to miss our 15 minutes of fame on the news. Trees twisted and snapped off at base like popsicle sticks after all cherry-ness has been sucked dry. Very sad. Glad we cut down big trees next to house two years ago. Have cereal and milk for breakfast. Dress warm. Glad we have wood-burning stove. Don't peek into freezer in garage, freezer in house. Picture what we want out of fridge. Snap it open, grab item, snap it shut. Need to see if world still out there. We drive to store. Gasp at massive damage along four miles between home and store. Trees down, power lines down, power poles down, must take a detour near store. Rural homeowners out with chain saws to clear roads. No power at QFC. Mark sings and dances down dark aisles. We giggle at high school girls coming around corner, doing same. They giggle at us. Bottled water still on shelves. We buy some. Dinty Moore beef stew, hot dogs, mangoes. Check on Erin's family in Bellevue. She is sick in cold apartment. Play with kids. "Sorry, no power" sign on Mark's doctor's dark door. No power anywhere. Loooong gas line at only station with power. Glad we filled up earlier. Head home. Pirates from city loading minivans with too many wood chunks that rural homeowners cut from trees blocking roads. Rural property owners good stewards. Pirates not knowing fresh wood no burny. Must season wood for a year. Hope city pirates get what they deserve—no heat.

Dec. 16 – More helicopters. Carry all items from fridge and freezer to camp coolers on front porch. 32 degrees outside. Milk will be OK. No peek in garage freezer. Cover it with big old carpet, black tarp, tie shut with camp rope. Say prayers for kids, power workers, city folk using grills indoors to stay warm! Can't communicate with kids, canceled cell phone due to disgust with carrier. "Emmy" the kitty climbed 60 feet up to tippy-top of pine tree hunting birdies or escaping coyotes, raccoons, and bears. Can't persuade her to come down. Steve brings more wood from shed. Sets up camp stove on front porch. Takes empty 5-gallon paint bucket down to creek and fills with water so we can flush saved up toilet items. We become the Clampetts. We attend the funeral of a dear friend. Generators power small lights in chapel. It is cozy, warm, and serene, despite the cold and sadness. We drive on to Erin's. Not home, leave note. She comes to our house at exact same moment we are at her empty house. Clampett family not home. Brother Nick drops in, finds sister Erin there. Both load up wood from the shed for their cold homes. Grandbabies disappointed Uncle Mark, Granny and Gramps Clampett not home, play chase outside to keep warm. We eat lunch at Steve's office in big city, make phone calls to family for first communications. Read paper about Storm of Century. See photos of massive damage around Puget Sound. Our neighborhood worst, worst by far. Charge laptop to watch movie later on at dark house for big entertainment value at time like this. Shop with Mark for engagement rings! Come home in dark. Take flashlights outside to try to coax Emmy out of tree. No. No comey down to cold house, tippy-top of pine tree in dark night must be warmer.

Dec. 17 – Heat water in pots on wood-burning stove. Take sponge bath. Dress for church. No one in parking lot. What? But we were here yesterday and it was OK! Mark says, "The storm beat God." Maybe someone left us message on phone that doesn't work not to come to church. Drive on small amount of gas left in tank to Nick's house. Surprise them with a few Christmas gifts. See giant tree that fell away from their house. Glad our prayers were answered. Nick's house on city water - take warm showers! Julie washes hair for first time in four days. Come home to find Emmy still crying in tree. Shake tree. Steve chain saws down tall skinny dead tree to use as Come Down Please Ladder for kitty. Three of us can't lift it. No phone to call Fire Department for help. No gas to drive to Fire Department for help. Wring hands. Shake tree hard. Emmy grips harder. Kitty friends "Bugs" and "Wiley" try to climb up to bring her down. Shoo! Dogs bark to call her down. Woof! No, no, meows Emmy. Last resort: Love little tree, love kitty more than tree. Say kitty prayer. Steve chain saws down Emmy's tree. Aims the tip over pile of deadfall so no squishy kitty. Emmy rides tree to ground! No squishy and proud of kitty! Jumps out, shakes off, gets land legs back after three days of gripping, races to dark, cold house for Ocean Wave Tuna. Insists on going back outside immediately after eating binge. On your own, sister! Toast aging bread on top of wood-burning stove. Eat mystery meat from porch. Play Scrabble by candlelight. For first time in 30 years Steve beats Julie in Scrabble. Uses word "quant." Julie challenges Steve's illegal word meaning "guy who works with numbers." Makes him look it up in big old fat dictionary. Disgusted to learn that "quant" is a real word! "A punting pole with flat cap at the end to prevent its sinking in the mud." 72 points on Triple Word Square. No hope of catching up.

Dec. 18 – Dental appointments. Always use bathrooms wherever we go. Get gas at only Bellevue station open. Premium $2.99 a gallon. Hurry and do things around house during daylight hours. Mark packs stuff for college, drives to Portland to ride with future father-in-law to see fiancée graduate from BYU-Idaho. Best excuse to get away from dark cold Fall City forest house! Eat from porch food. Steve wants to play Scrabble again. Julie beats him by 75 points. Go to bed early. We are in the Twilight Zone.

Dec 19 – Body clocks wake before dawn. Still stupefied. Julie drives into Fall City at noon. Still no power. Mail Flat Rate packages at dark post office as that's all they can accept. Check or cash only. Card machines no worky. Julie drives back into Fall City at 5 p.m. to pick up Steve from bus. Power on! Christmas lights on! Drives home. Power still off! No Christmas lights on! Clampetts still in Twilight Zone, not Beverly Hills, as hoped. Dredge more water from creek by flashlight. Flush aging toilet items. Roast aging hot dogs in wood-burning stove. Eat aging lettuce salad. Big aging candles burning lower, still dripping lots of wax. Intimate talk about buying generator. Daughter-in-law coming for Christmas in 4 days. Don't want her having to potty with bears in woods or in a Clampett wild totie. Very tired at 6 p.m. Go to bed at 8. Aging.

Dec. 20 – Steve goes worky. Julie prays for power. Many Christmas projects needing to be finished. Clean dry candle wax around living room, kitchen, bathroom. Tidy up disgusting Clampett house by daylight. Mumble about freedom for in-home chaos when power goes out. Cleans fridge for first time in 2 years. Scrapes old blueberry puddle from bottom of freezer. Spotless at 3:15 p.m. Ready for porch food. Stretches achy back and says out loud, "I'm ready!" like clean fridge is magic charm to solve all problems. Walks around house and says in most humble and sincere voice, "I'm ready! I'm ready! I'm ready!" More than ready for running water. Sits on floor to finish charcoal portrait of grandbaby. Listens to 106.9 Christmas music from small battery radio. Suddenly hears unusual noise. Snaps off radio with bated breath. WATER GURGLES IN TOILET TANK!!! LIGHTS COME BACK ON!!! DISHWASHER RESUMES CYCLE FROM 6 DAYS PREVIOUS!!! PRAYER HAS BEEN ANSWERED AT 3:44 P.M.!!! Powerful! Julie walks around house sniffling out loud, "Oh, Thank You!!!" First thing: flushes toilets. Resets dishwasher, stuffs big load of underwear into washing machine, turns on Christmas lights, rushes remaining aging porch food into spotless refrigerator, rushes to check on freezer full of food in garage. Still completely frozen!! Cleans toilets, turns on heater, marvels at all the luxuries in home. Marvels again and again. Gives thanks many times. Checks phone. No phone. That's OK! Begins to erase traces of Clampett house. Steve returns to happy house. Eat aging food from indoor refrigerator!! Julie too tired for shower.

Dec. 21 – Big long bubble bath! Phone works! 29 messages: "Are you OK? No church this week. Are you OK? Are you OK?..." Had we not been OK house would have stunk with moldering cold, maggot-ridden bodies and friends would have no need to drive to house wondering why no returny phone calls. Computer works! TV works! Kids and grandkids all safe and sound. See Mythbusters prove that hair spray holds Christmas tree needles on longer than any other special treatments. See 50,000 people still without power on local news broadcast. See power workers from California, Kansas, and Missouri here to help us flush toilets and have Merry Christmas. Sing old Glen Campbell song: "I am a lineman for King County, and I drive the main road, looking in Fall City for another overload..." Oh, lineman—I need you more than want you. And I want you for all time. And Wichita lineman, just stay on my line...da da da da da da.... Give thanks for luxury of good workers leaving own families at holiday time to give incredible service to strangers. Hurry, hurry to get Christmas projects done. Give thanks for luxuries. Give thanks for power. Give thanks for everything.
Main lesson learned: Next time power goes out in Fall City—must clean fridge immediately.

Dec. 22 – Maybe if all of us clean our fridges at exactly 3:15 p.m. on January 2, 2008, we can achieve World Peace. Powerful.

When it is dark enough, you can see the stars.
-Ralph Waldo Emerson

Water Fitness
2005

    The sesamoid bone in my right foot broke because I dropped it excessively.
    My first marathon is in October. I'll need my feet. But I whacked them too hard, just kept dropping them over and over again on the road, back and forth, in front of my house. You have to smack them like that when you run. I'm not sure what went wrong. Bad shoes? Hard pavement? Deadbeat bones? I didn't know it was broken and ignorance like this is not bliss. No matter—I'm not giving up this dream, this madcap affair, this nightmare, this running with the bizarros.
    To nurse my foot (didn't want to euthanize it) for this event, I limped over to the local YMCA for some water running, which is like water ballet, only upright, with a float belt to keep you from drowning, and without choreography, sparkly eye shadow, nose plugs, tight buns, or weirdness.
    I was terrified. A weak swimmer, with my share of body fat, but not enough to keep me afloat, I clutch flotation devices and cling to brisk respect for bottomless liquids. But I was most truly frightened to face the pod of old ladies who exercise there. This fear goes deeper than drowning. Varicose veins, potbellies, and balding heads, oh my!
    I was also scared to forsake training since I'd declared to people all spring that I was going to run a marathon. Once you commit to something out loud, you have to go for your goal or be totally embarrassed. Promises become real when you vocalize them. They will not be quiet and they will not be buried. When your ears register something new and surprising coming out of

your mouth, your brain has a hard time forgetting what it heard.

If I benefited from the old lady class, that would prove I was ancient enough to swim in the *Aquarobics* category. Or, heaven forbid, if I *enjoyed* the experience, I, beyond doubt, would *be* an old lady. 50 is the new 30...50 is the new 30...50's the new...

I stumbled across enough courage to drive to the Y, open the door, and walk in. Little-singing-mermaid-with-a-fork-in-her-red-hair, what's up with this? One youngish teacher and one student—age 13!—all chatty and friendly, from the shallow end they pointed the path to the float belts. I, the youngish thing in the deep end of the pool, didn't ask their names and they didn't ask mine. I did my water fitness thing and lived. Wow, that fear felt better.

So did my foot—a swift miracle, a complete cure, good enough to perform a new scientific experiment on the road. But the two-mile experiment failed because, wow, it hurt again; more than before. I guess one session in the water didn't cure my hurting bone. Um, duh. No pain, no gain, lose your brain, need a cane.

My second session in the pool was the bad dream come true. A different teacher, age...middle-ish...was shouting directions at 27 old ladies—age...ancient. Varicose veins, potbellies, balding heads, *and* flappy underarms. Oh, my! The coach's decibel level rose above this chattering, churning *pod* of old chums. With shaky hands I, feeble swimmer, applied the float belt to my waist and climbed down the ladder into the Twilight Zone.

There's nothing mysterious about water running. You make running motions, dangling chest-deep in yawning water that is not swallowing you down because you're wearing a Caribbean-colored girdle that keeps you floating. You don't have to tread, snort, or spit. Your contact lenses don't get chlorine-scorched. The water is warm for old bones, so the fearful event soothes you, charms you, lulls you into thinking that just *hanging* in warm water is vigorous exercise. Just *being* is good enough...*be* the water...be the water...be the water... You can float like Flounder. You can scamper like Thumper. You can flutter about like Tinkerbell.

Then, flick, ripple, surge...the pod scuttled around each other in two opposing circles, warming up, and here came the tsunami from the shallow end. Surf's up! My meditation was under attack. The ladies invaded my deep territory, forcing me to duck and run. They chattered during frog kicks, while I shrank into quiet laps around them. I didn't eavesdrop on purpose as I paddled past donkey kicks and dodged snow angels.

"...and my ice maker just won't stop. It keeps cranking and cranking. I've gotta get home and call someone, I guess. I don't know how to stop it," said the oldest lady in the pool, splashing past on her way to ab kicks. Where are all those ice cubes dropping? What does her kitchen floor look like right about now? Who should be catching them? She's 120 years old and in need of a plumber.

"He said with four daughters he had experimented with the first two on becoming a dad, and with the last two he could finally function. The first two weddings, he muddled around in a house filled with company. This time, he and Joanie rented a hotel room and left the house for the four girls!" Two gals giggled.

"He's got the right idea, you know..." They cross-country skied back to the gutter for push-ups, languid and laughing. I pictured Steve Martin in *Father of the Bride* before remembering the weddings of my two oldest children.

"But it doesn't sound like conjunctivitis," a curly brown hair with glasses said to her friend. "If she'll just keep a warm, wet cloth on it, it may help. You may want to get her over to the doctor's this week, though." I guessed she was a nurse and pictured my childhood pinkeye, gooey and crusty every morning for a week.

"You know, I've got to find something new to rinse out my swimsuit."

"I used to buy special soap for that, but when I ran out I just started using dish soap."

"Really?"

"Oh, it works just as well. I haven't noticed a difference. My suits last just as long. The other stuff you buy from department stores is so expensive."

"I just rinse mine out when I go into the shower. But then I've started to buy only nylon suits. They last so much longer than the Lycra."

Esther Williams floated through my mind, followed by her suave Fernando, then ice cubes, then wedding hotels...

"Back to the side for push-ups!" the instructor yelled again, grabbing her water bottle for a long swig. I didn't know you had to rehydrate during water workouts.

"Are you recuperating?" I realized the brunette was talking to me. I submerged Esther and Fernando, snapping back to aqua reality.

"Oh, yeah! I'm training for my first marathon in October and I have an old foot injury, kind of a painful tweak that I'm trying to mend. I need to keep up an equivalent cardio workout and muscle strengthening, the same running muscles..." I stroked backwards to keep my brief explanation from appearing snooty. Must keep the flow going for my endurance. "How 'bout you?"

"Oh, it's my knee," she grimaced, evading her froggy friends before following me.

"Oooohhhh," I grimaced back at her, dodging the white-haired lady who's been 16 for 64 years doing some really fierce froggies.

"Well, you're too young to have foot problems," she said. "You better be careful. If you don't take care of them now, they'll dog you forever."

"Yeah, well, I've been really careful and I'm hoping this will take care of it." To create more resistance in the water, mostly to gain speed, I ran away vigorously with flat palms. Monty Python was in my ear yelling *Run away! Run away!* and I felt bad that I didn't stay and chat with her, but I was going to be here only a few more times, so why get chummy?

"Why don't you join our class?" another white-haired one approached. She seemed kind and...kicky. Her hair was pulled back into a one-inch ponytail.

"Well, I'm training for my first marathon in October..." and I went into my spiel all over again. Voices carry well in pools, so didn't these gals all know by now that the rebel who wouldn't join cheerleader kicks was on a different course? Multitasking showoffs, they concentrated and waggled and jerked as they kibitzed.

"That's wonderful," she said. "Aren't marathons a long race?"

"26.2 miles."

"Oh, that's a long race!"

She wore a purple swimsuit. When I was 16, purple was not a real groovy color because hippies and Sonny and Cher wore lots of orange...and because we all knew there was a poem about being old and purple... *When I get old I'm going to be purple*...or wear it or something like that. My mind forced my brain to face the purple collection in my own closet. It surfaced like flotsam on a rocky shore. I gasped for air.

"Yes, it's very long, so I'm hoping to be careful and take care of this injury before it keeps me down any longer." I smiled and dipped away in polite inches.

Mary was today's instructor. Once everyone was awash in cheerleader kicks she spun over and gave me advice, showing me hearty cross-country ski motions to pump up my heart rate. She also gave me the name of her favorite podiatrist.

I hate to admit it, but ski strokes and foot man were the best advice I received all summer. I went to see her doctor and he took good care of me. Translation: X-rays. They revealed that maybe I was born with a puny sesamoid bone, or maybe I was carrying around an old dance injury, but *probably* it was my new wrong running shoes, so yummy on my feet it was like jogging in bunny slippers. Whatever...the sesamoid bone on the ball of my right foot was...fractured. Broken into zigzaggy halves. Um, duh. Why the heck didn't the on-call doc for our family physician take time to X-ray my slightly hurting foot and reveal this interesting fact two months ago? Instead, he looked bored and gave me a flat, stiff medical shoe to wear so I could "immobilize my foot for awhile." Thanks for compounding everything, doc.

I thanked Mary. With true validation for my long-standing pain, which was not an old tweak after all, but a new one, I wanted to *share* this fascinating knowledge with my old ladies. As horrifying as it seems—*as it is*—I swear, I could not help myself from *sharing* my medical history! Well, they asked how I was doing and that's my excuse. And upon overhearing about other foot problems in class, I referred Dr. S to two women, just minding their own business bicycling along in the deep end. Oh, I'm on my way to Purpleville.

The brunette with knee problems paddled over. "My name is Zandra," she said, "but everyone calls me Zee."

"Oh, cute name," I replied. "I'm Julie."

"Oh, like our other instructor. Her name is Julie, too, only it's J-u-l-i." Zee, with her infectious smile, her twinkly, crinkly eyes, made you wish you had known her for a long time.

We talked and paddled in a tight circle. I cross-country skied to the left for 45 minutes, wondered if my right side felt neglected, and pictured the special jeans I'd have to sew for my lopsided legs.

Every day's dunk into the pool was immersion into Zee's wonderful, horrible adventures as a former school teacher, or her world travels, or a fascinating plunge into her cultured mind.

"I want to find an excursion to Vermont this fall to see the leaves, but it has to be just the right tour." Would I be brave enough to travel alone? She left early, going back home to join an old college girlfriend visiting from the East Coast who was sleeping in, too sedentary to join her for some exercise at 8 a.m., which provoked eye-rolling from my friend. Then she was gone, and I was left, a solo dip.

After "cool down" in the shallow end with underwater bicep curls, one by one my classmates climbed up the ladder out of the pool. I watched potato-shaped bodies and curdled thighs drip water to the door marked "Women" and sighed. I felt more at home here than I felt I should, more at home than I ever, in a million years, thought I would.

A short gray-hair swam past and smiled at me warmly. "I'm Marion," she said without asking or advising.

"I'm Julie." I smiled back at her, aware that it had taken four sessions before four women out of 24 had spoken to me. But then, I hadn't spoken to many of them. *Why are you so shy and standoffish? So what if they're older? You're the youngest one in the pool; that should give you some confidence. You have the fourth least amount of cellulite.* I was the newest student, but age became my excuse for being shy. Without any reason to, I scuttled around in my own little bubble.

"...it's not like good Irish butter, you know...but then, there's nothing like good Irish butter..."

"I think you can get big barrels, food-grade barrels, to put water in."

"Maybe if we all move to Utah...I think we could find some emergency preparation items better there."

I volunteered, "We have two barrels at our house and we got them here."

When I told Sandy that I was on my way to the chiropractor straight from the pool, she said, "You better get going so you're not late." Then she apologized for "momming" me, like she does her husband sometimes.

"That's OK," I said. "I lost my mom 22 years ago and, you know, some days it's so nice to be 'mommed.'"

Steve swam with me on Friday, sleeping in and taking the day off. I made him come with me to class as a science experiment, as show-and-tell. He was nervous. "Won't they be mad that a man has come?" he asked.

"No, there's a little old token man who comes with his wife and no one is afraid of him."

"Yes, but, I am a manly man, a strange manly man who will flex his biceps at them and make them giggle."

"You do, that, Stud Muffin, and show them what they're missing."

On Monday, the class splashed through warm-up before Alan, the pool manager, came in. Because he was leaving to be a cop in Barrow, Alaska, the ladies sang and danced a watery *for he's a jolly good fellow.* He belly-flopped into the pool, crablike, bobbing up like a seal to shake the water off his head, and the lifeguard boy hit 'play' on the boombox. I cross-countried in the deep end as they all sang and splashed through "YMCA" with the Village People. They laughed and clapped for themselves while I clapped, too, alone in the deep end.

Do you ever get over the feeling that you don't fit in?

Reserved, distressed, left out, absurd, in the same water with old ladies, I mused *these pool days can be research for future projects.* Aware of my own snobbery, I forgave them theirs, remembering that occasionally, as a teen, I was accused of being snooty when what I was, was shy. I understand that these ladies are as bashful as I am. And though they're each here next to a friend talking nonstop, and have enjoyed this class for a long time, they're each busy with private thoughts, just as I am.

Shyness or distraction, the result is the same.

Bubbles, all of us, bobbing by on a skiff of water. Without eye contact, listening in as life floats us along, waiting to connect with a laugh or smile or doctor's referral, we are as transparent as bubbles, and just as delicate.

Don't poke at me and try to pop me.

I trained in this pool to protect my broken sesamoid bone. It's debatable whether this occurred. My admiration for, and dependence on, float belts increased proportionately to the atrophying of my swim strokes. I didn't receive one speck of sunshine or vitamin D on my white skin. Stroke by stroke, I paddled my way around this group, and in gleaning tiny kernels from these mature lives, something in me has been preserved, restored in these healing waters.

I used to look at these women as just old ladies. In reality, these women have flowing, Caribbean-colored hair. They are light, fluid mermaids trapped inside solid, aging, foreign bodies—Mrs. Potato Head bodies. Once out of the water and painfully heaving themselves up that skinny pool ladder, they emerge onto land fifty percent heavier. Don't be fooled, Mrs. Potato Head is just a disguise they wear.

It's OK with them that I'm not a mermaid, that this youngish person runs in a float belt. Like me, they are all athletes, recuperating. Like me, they are still 16. There is a freshness inside that you can sense. You feel their childhood more than see it, though if you look closely enough at their eyes you can see youth through the windows of older souls. These are more beautiful, complex, and interesting human beings. Recognizing this makes the observer a wiser human being. I wish I'd known this while my mom was still alive. She walked in disguise, too.

■   ■   ■

After six months and many wet cross-country skied miles, the big day in October arrived. Three days before we flew out for the marathon, Zee asked, "You'll keep coming the whole time before you go?"

"Yes," I said to her strange question, "but we're leaving Wednesday instead of Thursday."

"No! You told me you were leaving Thursday. Oh, I've made a big poster and I was going to put it up for you on Wednesday. A good luck poster. Oh dear."

"Oh, wow! That is so nice of you. I'm sorry, I re-checked my flight plans and it was a good thing, because our flight is on Wednesday not Thursday. I feel so bad. I'm sorry!" I meant it. I saw her genuine distress over my brain cramp with flight plans.

"If I had known I would have brought it today."

"I'll try to stop by Wednesday morning. I'll have enough time," I fibbed. Who ever has enough time before a flight? But I didn't want to disappoint my friend. "I'll swing by here with

Steve before we head to the airport." Steve and I will have to be organized enough to avoid making this a fib.

"Are you sure?" she disbelieved. She's a veteran of morning flights.

"I will make time to stop by for a few minutes," I promised. Through all the kicking and tight circles, Zee and I have become friends.

She stood shivering on deck in her dry swimsuit. A huge banner "Good Luck, Julie, October 1" hung on the wall. We hugged, happy for pools and signs and bubbles that can pass without popping. Juli snapped two quick pictures, hugged me, jumped into the water for warm ups and from the shallow end there were 24 *Good Lucks!* called out. Brown, gray, white hairs, in blue suits, black suits, and yes, purple suits, they smiled up at me and meant it.

"Good luck, and you take care of that foot." Zee looked worried, like she wanted to go with me, like my best friend Jeri would have looked at me, like my mom would have looked at me.

I had a two-part epiphany as we reached the airport. First: I've secretly loved purple my whole life, so after I'm done whacking my foot twenty-six point two miles, I'm hobbling straight to the store to buy a new swimsuit—lavender, lilac, violet, plum, amethyst, or even aubergine. Nylon, not Lycra. And I'm going to wash it in dish soap. Second: as I walked away from water fitness that day, I realized how unfit I was when I entered this pool. Now when I tell people I'm going to "My Old Lady Water Fitness Class" this title is an accolade, not an affront.

Long ago, my first smiley swim teacher in the shallow end said, "Don't be afraid, kids. Just slide down the steps there, hold onto the side, and let's blow *bubbles!*"

Old women are different from everyone else. They tell the truth.
-Ursula LeGuin

A half-truth is a whole lie.
-Jewish proverb

Home Ick and Recipes Betty Crocker Does Not Have
2005

    You never know when you're being an example to some twit skulking around in a sullen spasm.
    Home Ick was offered in my high school as a popular elective. I admired those girls who got involved. I really did. I admired the girls who modeled their "Make It Yourself With Wool" suits and jumpers and matching hats in Miss Broadbent's Home Economics spring fashion show and then actually wore their stuff afterward in real life. I admired the smells coming from Home Ec on my way to the gym. I admired the girls who won the "Betty Crocker Search for Tomorrow Homemaker Award" at the end of each school year—they got their 15 minutes of fame with a yearbook photo page devoted to them, plus a scholarship.
    Besides the satisfaction of knowing they had skills galore for their future homes and families, they were already, as teenagers, self-sufficient in genteel, practical, creative ways. They could survive an Idaho blizzard by deep-frying their own doughnuts while bundled up in handmade plaid jumpers, matching capes, and mukluks.
    I admired them so much, I wished they would come to my house and share their expertise with me. What I *honestly* mean is, I wished they would come to my house and whistle while they worked at doing my inside chores. I wished they could be my mom's daughter for a few hours each week. Tomboys would rather muck out a horse stall than take Home Ick or do inside chores.
    Now that I've been around the block a few times with vinegar and a wad of paper towels and watched others shine brighter than me, I may have missed my calling...

First - *Ordinary* people with bad taste and haughty attitudes (both of which are admired by masses of people) make big money designing horrid clothes that the masses pretend to like. The masses trade their hard-earned money for the skimpy, skanky clothes created by the haughty ones. The masses trade at least *10 hours* of life bagging fast food in exchange for the latest *cheap* tissue baby T-shirt that doesn't cover a belly button. Because the masses didn't take Home Ec and don't sew, they have no choice but to buy and wear stuff they'd rather not, fashioned by people who obviously didn't take Home Ick, who call themselves "Designers." Where is Miss Broadbent when you need her? That's what you get for being a non-sewer.

Second - *Privileged* people are invited to poke around in drawers that don't belong to them, handle personal items that don't belong to them, and organize closets that don't belong to them. They get paid lots of money for poking, handling, snooping and bossing other people and other people's stuff because they call themselves "Organizational Experts." They could be called "Your Mom." That's what you get for being a slob.

Third - *Tricky* people call themselves "Life Coach." They charge scads of money to boss clients into doing things they already know they should be doing. When I was 9 I used to do this to my 6-year-old brother. Except he never did pay me, he hardly ever did what I told him around to do, and he called me "dumb bum stupid sister" before going off to play Batman and Robin with his friend Scott. That's what you get for being a sibling.

Final example - *Über-tricky* people, or "Say So's," have such a large army of Future Homemakers of America working for them that the über-trickies make millions of dollars, sometimes serve time in jail for various reasons, then come back out and make millions more. We do things because they "Say So." It's what I wanted to do about my inside chores as a teenager, except not the jail part. I was not clever enough to become über-tricky. Don't be fooled by these types, their pretty stuff, and their trends. They command armies that you and I don't have. That's what you get for being simple.

Today Betty Crocker is frantically searching for her Homemaker of Tomorrow Award recipients—her self-sufficient warriors of yesteryear. *Where has all the flour gone? Long time passing...Where have all the homemakers gone? Long time ago-o-*

o... Sing this sad ballad with your guitar, call yourself Lone Spoon, and wait for your noodles to stick to the wall, my people.

I escaped Home Ick by taking drama classes. And by participating in 4-H during the summer, like most country kids do, I could escape inside chores for awhile by visiting the next farm over to learn inside chore gunk from young adult women who I admired. I learned how to sew from my sister-in-law, Mary Ann. (and my mom). I learned how to knit from Martha, a dairy girl three farms over and good friend of the family (and my mom). I learned how to crochet and embroider as a malleable child in Primary and Young Women's—two youth auxiliaries in our church (OK, OK, and from my mom).

For me, the creative factor inherent in these dainty arty skills outweighed the sissy factor. But a little needlework goes a long way. My 9-year-old fingers allowed the threads to get knotty so fast, and when my threads were knotty, I was naughty with silent swearwords inside my head like "Dang you, blue floss!" I quickly hated embroidery. That's what you get for saying silent Dangs.

Somehow tomboys learn to be homemakers. My mother didn't know it, but I watched her even as I blew raspberries at all her amazing accomplishments. I mocked the joy she found in it. I was ungrateful about the nurturing, comforting service she provided to her family.

Mom inadvertently taught me to bottle peaches and strawberry jam, dust books, make cinnamon rolls, and sew prom formals—all as a skulking twit having tantrums about being trapped inside. Instead of always being allowed to roam outside, like an Indian maiden or a wild cowgirl, (whichever I felt like on that particular day) and ride my horse, climb my cottonwood tree, or, at age 12, drive the tractor for my brothers bucking hay bales, I was asked to come inside to help and—dang it!—learn homemaking skills. That's what you get for having no sisters. Where's a sister when you need her?

One autumn day 20 years later, Mom came into my own kitchen and saw 28 quarts of peaches sparkling in Mason jars on my counter. "When did you learn how to bottle peaches?" she asked, trying hard to keep the incredulity out of her voice.

"Oh, I was watching you the whole time," I said as I nonchalantly wiped homemade applesauce off my baby's chin. She gasped in amazement and her mouth hung open all day. That's what you get for being a mother.

So, you just never know when you are being any kind of example. Thank heavens my mother was a well-rounded, wonderful example, even though she wasn't a kindred tomboy when I knew her. As a farm wife and mom who worked outside the home so we could eat 49-cents-a-pound hamburger, she didn't have time to be a tomboy when I knew her. Now that she's been gone for 23 years and I've done lots of growing up without her, my thick head has realized that she had her own share of tomboy adventures. I'm sorry I didn't know her then. I'm sorry I never gave her credit for being adventurous and fun.

I first suspected her hidden past one hot July day when my mother, my brothers, and 12-year-old me floated down our irrigation canal together. When we clambered up the muddy, grassy bank to run back for another float down on the swift current, my mother discovered six brown leeches clinging to her right leg and four brown leeches clinging to her left. We gasped at the monsters on our mother. She pulled them off, laughing, as they stretched out long before snapping off her wet skin. Her children "eeewwww-ed" in awe at her bravery, and in disgust and disappointment at not having any of our own gross creatures sucking the life out of us. She didn't even scream. A true tomboy sign.

Tomboys are fond of interesting combinations, riveting situations, and dangerous multitasking…like playing dolls by smushing barn kittens into Barbie clothes; like shooting big old hornoobus green peas from your slingshot at a skunk invading the garden; like running with scissors and pliers to rescue the family dog from porcupine quills.

We're partial to scientific experiments. Tie a dreaded tobacco-spittin' grasshopper to a firecracker next time you celebrate the Fourth of July. It's an interesting method of pest control. Pick up a blow snake by the tail and chase the little brother who won't obey your bossing. I can show you Mumblety-peg scars on my shins from games we played on the back lawn with Boy Scout knives when we were supposed to be pruning the lilacs. Tomboys are not sissies. But we can be braggarts.

Dramatic recipes with fascinating mixtures attract tomboy attention. Like an old Mepps spinner to a Brook trout, enthralling recipes lure tomboys to kitchens, and like a barbed hook, uniquely gripping events are what keep us there. So, to touch the hearts of tomboys everywhere, and for those of you who only dream of being one, and in honor of my mother, I share a few of my riveting recipes—genu-i-ne concoctions from Pioneers, Mountain Men, Homesteaders, Homemakers, and Other Hardy Types. Miss Broadbent, you would be so proud. Betty Crocker has not placed these in her cookbook. Betty Crocker, even though we love her, is frightened by these recipes. Betty Crocker is a sissy.

Canned Fish
Clean and fillet fish. Pack pieces in sterilized pint jars. Add ½ teaspoon salt and 1 tablespoon butter. Pressure at 10 pounds for 90 minutes or 2 hours for whole fish in quarts. *(This sounds much easier than it really is. First you have to catch the fish, which means you have to dig worms for bait and then you have to thread the worms on your hook in such a way that they do not jump off once they hit the cold rushing river water. Then you have to catch the fish, which requires lots of patience. Once you catch them you have to clean them. Fisherperson vernacular is "gut them," which means you, in polite terms, well, you know what this means. With some practice, you can learn to do this in one smooth motion. Trust me, it's easy. I was 7 when I learned how. Then you have to have the right type of knife for filleting, a sharp one, to take out all the bones in one clean swipe. This is not easy. You don't want dinner guests choking on some little overlooked canned fish bone. See what I mean? And we haven't even talked about "pressure" yet. Although this is a recipe with only three ingredients, maybe you should just buy that Sorry Charley stuff in the supermarket. That's what I do today. Otherwise I'd have to be in the kitchen pretending I know what "pressure" means. I'd rather be outside with worms.)*

Mustard Plaster (for croup)
1 egg white   2 to 3 T. flour
1 T. dry mustard
Mix. Put on sterile cloth and fold over. *(A pita sandwich.)* Put on chest or back as long as they can stand it. *(Well, this is very clear. You may not want to wear this yourself, but "they" will.)*

Mentholatum-Type Stuff
1 lb. petroleum jelly   ¼ oz. menthol crystals
2 (1 oz.) cakes camphor, shaved with a knife
Melt petroleum jelly and camphor in top of double boiler. *(This is an exciting recipe since there's a knife involved, but I know*

double boilers cause twice the trouble one pot does, so be careful. CAUTION! Once I melted caramels in the top pot of a double boiler, thinking I had put water in the bottom pot. I had not. And when I set the hot pots down in the MIDDLE of my family room floor to let my kids gather round and dip apples in a joyful bohemian snack, in a split second my hot pot melted the beautiful wall-to-wall cream-colored carpet. None of my tomboy recipes tell me how to revive a perfectly round, melted nylon circle in the middle of a rental-home rug.) Add menthol crystals and stir until dissolved. Pour into small jars and seal tightly.

Homemade Soap

1 can lye　　　　　　　　　½ c. ammonia
1 qt. hot water　　　　　　 ½ c. bleach
2 qts. hot grease　　　　　 4 heaping T. Borax

The fat in this recipe should be clean. To do this, put fat in water, bring to a boil and let stand until fat is set. Then remove the hard fat. *(Well, if it was this easy to remove hard fat we'd all look like Audrey Hepburn.)* Dissolve the lye in hot water. Add hot fat, Borax, bleach and ammonia to water; add lye/water mixture and stir constantly for 5 minutes. Stir every 15 minutes until it powders. *(Don't ask me, I don't know. You lost me at clean fat.)* Use only an enamel pan to make this. Also this may be made into bar soap by letting it stand until cool after the first stirring.

Play Dough

1 c. flour　　　　　　　　　　　　¼ c. salt
1 tsp. salad oil (or alum)　　　½ c. water with color

Use salad oil or alum—according to taste. *(I just threw those last three words in to see if you were paying attention. Someone in your household will want to eat this. Someone who also likes to eat grade school paste. Maybe you. See the disclaimer.*)* Knead until workable. If you want a stiffer dough, add more salt. Store in quart jar in refrigerator. *(There are new inventions now called Tupperware. My mother burped her Tupperware. Are we still supposed to burp our Tupperware?)*

Cooked Play Dough

1 c. water　　　　　　　　　　1 c. flour
2 T. oil　　　　　　　　　　　 ½ c. salt
2 tsp. cream of tartar　　　 food coloring

Mix in pan and cook until mixture pulls away from side and forms a ball. *(This one is for you showoffy types who won the Betty Crocker Search for Tomorrow Homemaker Award and will not be satisfied with uncooked play dough.)*

So, to recap:

1. Mountain Men pampered themselves more than they let on.

2. Good news! Home Ec was a required block for my sons and my daughter in junior high. Because of this our future is preserved.

Speaking of preserved—when I set the glass jars of peaches, cherries, and tomatoes on my pantry shelves, the glowing reflections I see in those jewel-tones are the faces of my mother and my grandmothers, all gone now. They're smiling with contentment because their tomboy is carrying on (in a good way).

We are more alike than not. That's what you get for just being.

For all that I thought I knew about these women of my heritage, the ripe abundance I preserve tells me there is depth that I don't know of yet. For every bottle of rhubarb jam I place there with my own hands, there remain the mysteries—trees, horses, canals, games, dreams, disasters—that belong to them. Someday we'll all sit down again together and glory over lost treasures. If they cook, it'll be heavenly. I will enjoy every morsel.

*Disclaimer: Do not eat the results of these recipes. They might kill you. Do not feed them to your family either. Mountain Men are all dead now and what does that tell you? Don't do stupid things with these special recipes and then pretend you're sick from them, or dead, and then try to sue me. You can, however, feed them to your leeches.

Why does Sea World have a seafood restaurant?? I'm halfway through my fish burger and I realize....I could be eating a slow learner.

-Lynda Montgomery

Just a Little Poke
2004

Dear Victoria,

Remember how betrayed you felt when you were a little whippersnapper and the doctor giving you your booster shots said it would be *just a little poke*? Yeah, me too. Using this subtle scheme picked up from medical professionals, it's my duty to convince Steve that he's about to receive *just little poke*. Why? Because he's really having a C-section.

Steve was hoping for the new robotic laparoscopy procedure, but evidently the wee babe he's grown is the largest one ever known to mankind—something we should be proud of—a vast unit three times normal size. Had we been glory hounds, to document this birth we'd have invited the official measuring people from *Guinness World Records*.

Here in the hospital, these medical types are picky about who wanders in and out of their rooms. No doulas in surgery. I'll tell you from previous doula experience that we are not always welcome in the operating room during a C-section, though we should be. Welcomed with gracious arms, a bag of chips and a milkshake. Yeah, and a pony! It's a proven scientific fact that simply having a doula in the birthing room shortens the time a mom is in labor, helps nurses breathe easier, and lowers hospital costs. *Plus,* doulas stay on their feet whispering strong words of encouragement to the birthing mother—constant reminders of mom's physical, psychological and emotional power. Mom's enabled to shut the gate on pain while dads are shutting their fingers in gates, plummeting to, and puking on, floors.

I suspect all this man behavior in hospitals is not so much about sharp scalpels as it is about the fear of involuntary "happy place" secrets leaking out because they might be unconscious. *I'd tell you where my favorite fishing hole is, but then I'd have to kill you.*

Men can be scared, *varry varry* scared, about stuff *not* found on the garage workbench.

When Nick broke his hand sliding into third base off his great triple slam, Steve persuaded Nick and me to "sleep on it overnight" and if the hand still hurt in the morning we would visit the doc. Being the plucky, patient, quietly stoic child that he'd always been, 15-year-old Nick looked me in the eye (we both *knew* it was broken), trusted that Dad would come to his senses, swallowed the aspirin I gave him, grimaced as I propped his hand under ice on a pillow on his chest, and then tried to sleep. Guess how successful that was? In the morning his poor, painful hand had ballooned to the size of his baseball mit.

I don't know if Nick was mad at his dad, but *me* sure was. Me varry, varry mad.

We three drove to the doctor's office, scrutinized Nick's X-ray parading two clean diagonal breaks in two bones in front of you-know-who's nose, then drove to the hospital. While two of us read stale magazines, party No. 3 was in surgery. Nick still sports three metal bone screws; but as far as I know, his hand keeps quiet through airport security.

When our babies were tiny, Steve, squeamish, had to leave the room before pediatricians poked them with immunizations and jaundice tests, while I held them, *doula*ing them before I even knew what the word meant. Moms are not sissies.

Squeamy-Dads are a fact of life. And yet they'll refuse medical intervention and set their own broken fingers when they need to. Go figure. When was the last time the man you know went for a complete medical checkup? Truth be told—there are lots of dads who are more tender about their families than about themselves. (And protective about insurance costs and family finances.) Dads cannot afford to be wussies.

So this morning it was appropriate that I folded Steve's clothes into the hospital bag, tattled about the Cold-Eeze he popped to stop his cough during his pre-op fast, and held his hand. He kept a tight smile on his face as white-coated people swarmed him like mosquitoes. I know him well enough to know he'd rather perform his own surgery himself. While Nurse Carolyn inserted his IV, I doula-rubbed his arm and smooched him goodbye. Dr. Silverman gave me the heave-ho before wheeling Steve out of the room. In a quiet-spoken, non-drinking, non-druggy man, you know the IV meds are crackin' when, thirty seconds under anesthesia, he recalls our trip to the Kona coast in a voice so loud the receptionist down the hall hears surfboards crashing, and laughs so hard at his funny tales that the milk she's nursing with her bran muffin squirts out her nose.

"Well, I hope he doesn't spill any family secrets," I said.

Dr. S grinned at me, "He's gone to his happy place." You gotta love a doc who talks like that.

Like other C-sectioned moms, Steve's recovery period will drag on for six weeks. Not the happy place. The laparoscopy recovery would have taken only two weeks. Darn. In more ways than one...

A couple years ago, on his road to recovery from jaw surgery, after I dragged the still drugged up Steve home from the hospital and into our house, all he could do for a month was just lie around and not open his mouth wider than a straw's width. I actually *wanted* to dote on him as post-op doula, beyond normal wifely stuff. I had dug up healthy recipes for fruit shakes, nutritional supplement shakes, veggie shakes, soy shakes, avocado shakes, even refried bean with salsa Tex-Mex shakes! But he growled at me from deep in his throat (you heard that serious kind of snarl from other dogs before you chose to adopt Muttley the mixed Lab) and refused my help. My big 6'4" he-man was reduced to craawwwling out of the easy chair, clutching our afghan around his shoulders like a little old man model. You see this during New York Fashion Week when the bony, slump-shouldered girls strut out the season's new wraps. He'd shuffle into the kitchen and feebly paw through the cupboards, mumbling something through his wired jaw like, "Gaw boo." Translation: something about canned liquid nutrition and constipation. Mr. Grouchy Pants.

I finally threw up my hands, grilled myself a T-bone, and devoured it in front of him.

Major puniness is not going to be tolerated by the doula this time around, buster! He's promised me that he'll be a better patient. How is that possible with a 20-foot catheter taped into his private parts for three weeks to drain his private fluids? How is that possible with a humongous stapled incision, itchy as soon as he gets home? If he's not a happy camper, and he does become Mr. Grumpy Pants, I'll not just escape to steak; I'll escape to spa and crawl into mud.

Anyway, right now Steve is under general anesthesia with an epidural in his back spurting in lovely, numbing morphine. By now he's achieved the big incision—from his belly button all the way down to his pubic bone. Ah, C-sections. But hey, there is good news: we're having a boy!

A boy so unusual we haven't named him yet. No slapping of a teeny cute bottom to make it cry. No Carter's footy sleeper dotted with blue teddy bears. No picture-snapping by the proud family. No bubble-gum cigars in the waiting room for your fellow women, spinning on pins and nail beds, waiting. No paparazzi, no mamarazzi. No koochy-koochy cutesy stuff because what's coming out is a rogue, a maverick, a traitor, a brat. It's a freak of nature. Something we should pickle in raspberry vinegar to display on the kitchen counter. Replace the big glass decanter full of yellow lemons.

Oh, and I should break it to you gently now, I guess. I have prostate cancer. Birthing men and prostate cancer women—has the world gone mad?

Right now I'm in the waiting room on the surgical floor. It's huge and bright, and trying to convince all of us that our cares are not. Several women are here, waiting on their big, ol' men, birthing out poisons of various sizes through C-sections. Steve is under the scalpel for a radical prostatectomy. I have a few hours to…(please, not kill), a computer on my lap, and a big echoey canyon ricocheting around my sternum. For if your husband has prostate cancer, you have it, too.

Oh, hey, Dr. Pelman is coming, gotta go…OK, I'm back…two hours later, after a doctor visit and some lunch. But this afternoon is dragging on way too long. At noon, Dr. P said the operation went well and Steve was leaving recovery and on the way back to his room; so I've moved up to the waiting area on Steve's floor. But he's not back in his bed yet and he's overdue by an hour and a half. My canyon echoes.

Right, well, I'll just keep talking to you, dear friend.

We found out about this new medical adventure the morning K.C. flew home from Chile. It had been two years since we'd seen our son, who had put his college life on hold, and paid his own way so he could serve a mission for our church. So when the nurse called from the doc's office in her hushed voice, wanting us to come hear the news in person, Steve said *"nah."* He knew the results before the biopsy was ever taken. She kindly confirmed it over the phone. Like we couldn't guess from her invitation that it was bad news. While our kids and grandkids finished painting the *¡Hola! Welcome Home!* posters, noisy and excited to greet their beloved brother and uncle, Steve and I slipped upstairs to the master bathroom, and silently held each other.

"For the next couple days, let's just put *it* on hold and concentrate on K.C.'s welcome home," he said.

Toss out ideas about Squeam-Dads.

Since then we've been doing our cancer homework, eating lots of stuff with lycopene in it, choosing the surgeon and the right procedure for Steve's baby. He's had a bone scan, which revealed that the rest of his body is free of cancer. Because he's young, (ha! at 54! *relatively young*, they qualified) the docs wanted to remove the prostate through nerve-sparing surgery in order to prevent any cancer from escaping outside the membrane into his bloodstream. So, my friend, once Dr. P births this baby, medical people, not *Guinness* people, will weigh it, measure it, spank it, and biopsy it to see if it has been contained. We are counting on this.

My only moment of true fear (besides this overdue moment right now) was in Dr. P's office, when he was reassuring Steve and me about his high rate of success with this kind of surgical treatment. The frog in my throat was Calaveras County quality—the big C—*it* suddenly became real. And I had the biggest urge to give Dr. P the Three Stooges eye poke.

In hindsight, we should have paid more attention, earlier attention, to Dinah, our brilliant but rowdy Airedale terrier. Before Dr. P entered the picture, Steve was forced to sneak (unsuccessfully) through our front door from work, rush upstairs, and change into his jeans before coming down to get attacked by the dogs. We thought Lucy was just doing her job being a licky, lappy Jack Russell when she insisted on climbing into his lap (a no-no) the minute he sat down. Dinah would stick her snout onto his fly like it was coated with liver paté. Excited to play patty-cake with Daddy, she'd scratch at his crotch with both paws, digging for truffles or dark chocolate or diamonds. In reality we had a big, smart cancer-sniffing dog in our home concerned about the family jewels. We now watch clever canines like ours on evening magazine shows and wonder why we don't license our pooches as medical assistants.

OK, Dr. P was just here again—*finally*. Steve's blood pressure dipped so low in recovery, it got dangerous. They monitored him very closely for a long while, but he's on his way back up to his room now...for real. A green meadow has grown, filling my empty canyon. So I'll finish quick now and go kiss the new C-sectioned parent of our no-good baby boy.

Long story short: our kids and their babies will have Thanksgiving with us, our cousins, and all their babies. Our man of honor, Steve, will preside on the sofa in the special recovery outfit I purchased for his catheter convenience. It won't rub, itch, or bind: a blue plaid ladies flannel nightie, size XL, with white picot lace adorning collar and cuffs. Watch for pictures coming your way. Between all that's happened and all that's going to happen, I don't know when I'll have time to get Christmas ready. I need an elf or two. Are you sure you don't want to come for a little visit? Ha ha.

Thanks for listening, my friend. Gotta go now.

Oh! I just thought of a good masculine name for Steve's big bad boy baby— Blob.

P.S.,

It's taken me six weeks to post this letter. You, the most kind-hearted dog lover I know, will be interested to learn that our terriers no longer have any desire to paw at Daddy's crotch. The moment Blob came out, the dogs lost interest. The real jewels are safe. Blob, that masked-marauder-manpart is no longer, and the dogs are at peace with their world.

P.P.S.,

Auntie Victoria, don't ever tell Blob I spoke about him so harshly. Labels can be so destructive.

I will have no man in my boat who is not afraid...
-Starbuck in *Moby Dick*, first mate
on the doomed *Pequod* whaling ship

Life is not separate from death. It only looks that way.
-Blackfoot proverb

At every single moment of one's life, one is going to be no less than what one has been.
-Oscar Wilde

Fear less, hope more; whine less, breathe more; talk less, say more; hate less, love more; and all good things are yours.
-Swedish proverb

The Daring Young Girl on The Flying Trapeze
2005

Have you always wanted to run away and join the circus? Maybe you want to do it right now. What if you knew you were already there?

Are you burdened today with loads of care? Financial pressures, stress, abuse, loss of a loved one? Have you been touched by chronic illness, cancer, AIDS? Do you worry about future calamities? Have you tried to exercise faith but felt no benefit and feel that heaven may be shut tight against you?

If you and I could sit down with a glass of cold milk and some warm cookies and discuss our list of trials, we might categorize them—tons of slivers and bruises, lots of broken bones, and a few near-death experiences.

In the summer of 1995, Steve and I take our four children to Whistler, B.C., for a short family vacation. We find some fun activities, including a huge trapeze apparatus run by real circus pros. I don't know about you, but I've always wanted to fly on a trapeze. Maybe you'd prefer to stick your head into a lion's mouth or squish yourself into a tiny clown car with twenty-six other knuckleheads. Not me. I would cheer and clap for your circus tricks, but let me go up high and fly.

The six of us join a crowd gawking at pre-adolescent kids trying out circus life on this outdoor summer trapeze. I am drawn to the grounded adults. All the mommies and daddies gaze up into the heavens above the net, slack-jawed, a wistful gleam in their eyes, big flashing sign gleams that shout I REALLY WANT TO DO THIS! The children are good examples of I AM DOING THIS! But the adults all hold back. Only one little girl connects with the acrobat straining to catch the kids one after the other.

My palms begin to sweat. After two minutes of this agonizing sweaty rapture I smack Steve on the arm and say, "I have to try this." I've never been so close to such an open invitation to circus adventure. As I watch brave kids try and fail, and longing adults transfixed but timid, I know I will always regret it if I don't try to fly.

I give my $10 bill to Jeanetta, who, in her lovely French accent, talks me through very detailed instructions for being on their flying trapeze. Adrenaline kicks in as I climb the ladder—fourteen inches wide with rungs the diameter of an Oscar Mayer wiener. I get tired immediately and it hurts my bare feet! Twenty feet up the ladder I think, *my arms are tired, too. What if I don't even make it up this ladder and I humiliate my children?* At thirty feet up I think, *perhaps tiny Jeanetta will have to climb up here behind me and carry me on up...or down.*

At forty feet up I climb out onto a platform the size of a snowboard, landing shoulder to shoulder with Rocko, the Platform Guy. He buckles up my safety harness, repeating the very detailed instructions Jeanetta gave me hours ago down below. I love heights, but as I stand there quivering, I think, *This is scarier than it looks!* Philippe, the third French Canadian circus pro, sits easily on the opposite trapeze 100 feet away, swinging and smiling at me as I promise to obey their very detailed instructions.

Rocko yells out to Philippe, "Hup!" That's trapeze talk for *start swinging!* I perch on tippy-toes at platform edge as Philippe dangles by his knees, swinging gracefully on his trapeze; and when Philippe reaches some mysterious point with his timing, Rocko says, "Okayyyy, now!" I feel him lift my harness slightly and nudge my backside to ensure that I don't stall and ruin our professional circus timing.

It takes about four seconds to swing out from the platform and back again. Four seconds in which to bring your legs up and over the bar, grip it with your knees, let go with your hands, and swing upside down...waiting. Without seeing him, I trust that my partner, Philippe, is there somewhere with good timing.

Another two seconds to arch your back and neck, swing away once more, hold up your arms (whatever direction that is now), look for Philippe, and stretch out your hands so he can grab your wrists. Wanting that connection desperately, I strain even the muscles *between* my fingers. I never see Philippe.

But, miraculously, my puny amateur strength is enough and our timing is perfect. As I feel Philippe's strong, reassuring grip on my wrists, he whispers "I've got you." Jeanetta and Rocko shout, "Let your knees go!" My family cheers way down below, snap photos in wild abandon, and then there's some other loud screaming. Screams actually coming from my own mouth—"This is so much fuuuunnnnn!"—as I fly through the air with the greatest of ease.

Philippe swings with you once, twice, and then flips you with a twist back to your own trapeze. In the rushed, dangling blur, I can't see what I'm reaching for and I miss it. So Rocko lowers me to the net on the harness rope. I grab the edge and flip to the ground like a real circus woman. Your $10 lets you go up once more for another try.

Philippe and I connect again. Again, I miss the return bar. Back on the ground, though, Jeanetta presents me with their certificate for completing the "Hanging Knee Catch" and says after I rest up, I get to try a harder maneuver. Thankfully, we have spent our last cash and I am exhausted.

The next day I can barely walk or move my head. I had used *every single* muscle in my body. On the back of both knees lie bruises the size of 12-inch Subway sandwiches. The kids take more pictures—evidence of my joy and my pain. Evidence of opposition in *all* things.

I hate to live with regrets and don't much care for bruises. So this causes me to ask you: How often are we *spiritually* transfixed and timid? Often as the world seems topsy-turvy dark and heaven seems far away, we like to blame everything around us when the real cause of pain and fear may be our lack of faith in our Savior, Jesus Christ.

I love our scripture ancestors. Do you ever ponder that our leatherbound ancestral scripture family had lists of painful wounds just like ours? Scriptures are The Big Journal of their afflictions. If we study people like Esther, Job, Deborah, Thomas, Abish, Lehi, Sariah, Joseph and Emma, how can we not believe we'll be healed as they were? How did they triumph? It wasn't by having faith in faith, faith in happy endings, faith that every dark cloud would have a silver lining, or faith that time would heal all wounds.

Time doesn't heal any wounds, the Savior does. Our ancestral people had faith in the Lord Jesus Christ and a deep conviction that God, our Heavenly Father, knows us personally, loves us, hears our prayers and answers our prayers with what is best for us.

Like Amulek, there was a time in my life when "I did harden my heart, for I was called many times and I would not hear; therefore I knew concerning these things, yet I would not know; therefore I went on rebelling against God, in the wickedness of my heart..."* even as I knew the gospel of Jesus Christ was true, served in church callings, was a good wife and mother. In that lifetime ago, I was spiritually immature, with lots of good intentions, scratching the surface as a disciple, a latter-day "saint," not truly understanding the detailed instructions of faith.

Adversity can increase faith or it can be the cause of bitterness. I had gone through some serious trials angry and proud and asking "why." Because He loved me, the Lord compelled me to be humble, and painfully, rung by rung, I struggled through some much-needed repentance until I had more confidence in the Lord, a truer faith, and more courage.

I'm still climbing rung by rung. And now I know that sometimes we need the Lord's nudge from our precarious, comfy platforms so that we can take a leap of faith.

All those trials prepared me for the next, harder maneuver: my dear brother—a returned missionary of The Church of Jesus Christ of Latter-day Saints, who, as an assistant to the mission president in Thailand, helped translate the Book of Mormon into the Thai language—lay dying of AIDS. Just three years after returning from Thailand he fell away from the gospel he loved, confiding in me: *Life was just too hard – I gave up.* He missed the bar and felt too exhausted to climb back up the ladder.

The blessing of adversity *plus* a broken heart and contrite spirit equals greater power. Entering the home of my dying brother, I was physically all alone, but I entered encircled with an armor of light—the spiritual fortification I so needed in order to attend his death, plan his funeral, and finish the details of his life. Never before had I felt this way in the *middle* of a trial.

My puny amateur strength was enough. And so, at this exquisite high point of personal pain, the Lord grabbed hold of me in midair, catching me so that I did not fall, silently whispering, *"I've got you"* and I was carried with exquisite peace. As you well know, life goes on, and this experience with the Lord prepared me for the next, more difficult trial.

Faith grows as it is tested...only IF. Any person flying on a trapeze may believe that she can successfully fly through stormy skies alone, but unforgiving natural laws will convince her otherwise—with bruises.

IF we have the desire...I REALLY WANT TO DO THIS!...then we trust God enough to obey his detailed instructions. We acknowledge that it is not "the universe" that blesses us, it is God, and we offer gratitude for each blessing, however small. We seek the Lord and wait on his timing. We humbly pray, act on intuition, conscience, but especially the personal revelation He sends us through the still, small voice. We study the scriptures and serve others; worshipping this way every day or we become weak and miserable. Faith grows as we test the integrity of the safety harness.

We practice patience as God lets us struggle to grab higher bars that we keep missing. As we act courageously, our confidence grows; we can feel rested between blurry dangles; our faith muscles, once our weakness, strengthen; and then faith becomes our power—vibrant and unshakable—and we find ourselves screaming, "This is so much fun!"

Intentions are vapor clouds in your high trapeze atmosphere. I know that if we always *mean* to read the scriptures, *mean* to have personal and family prayer, *mean* to gather our family together once a week for home evenings, *mean* to serve others with love—it's a poor, *mean* way to treat our divine eternal selves, God our Heavenly Father; and his Son, Jesus Christ. The best of intentions leave us with restlessness, a gnawing ache that will not go away until we act upon our faith, choosing to put the kingdom of God first in our lives. When we dare to climb and stretch, in spite of pain and fear, if we grab the bar and leap, we will safely soar in the arms of the Lord.

My witness to you is this—like Alma: "I do not boast in my own strength, nor in my own wisdom; but behold my joy is full, yea, my heart is brim with joy, and I will rejoice in my God. Yea, I know that I am nothing; as to my strength I am weak; therefore I will not boast of myself, but I will boast of my God, for in his strength I can do all things..."*

Being that strong, we have no need, no desire, to run away.

* (These references are found in *The Book of Mormon: Another Witness of Jesus Christ*.)

The great danger for most of us is not that our aim is too high and we miss it but that it is too low and we reach it.
-Michelangelo

BoomerTweener™
1989 to Present Day

One day Nick was shootin' at some food and up from the ground come a'bubblin'…no wait…that's another story.

On Nick's twelfth birthday we gave him a compound bow just his size so he and Steve could deer hunt together. (Now don't get all uppity about hunting. It's what kept your ancestors alive so you could be here today. And whether you understand it or not, it's what keeps food on *your* table.) They helped other Boy Scouts achieve the Bow and Arrow Merit Badge on the road to becoming Eagle Scouts. With hours of practice, they both became very accurate.

One day Nick was target shooting and for some odd reason (maybe he knew I wanted to serve celery for dinner that night) he turned back toward the house to park his last arrow in the middle of the lawn. We watched him through our six by ten foot picture window, which framed Mount Timpanogos so beautifully. From thirty feet away he let fly the arrow and…

It ricocheted off the lawn. We watched that projectile coming toward the house in slow motion, like a 3-D scene between Peter Pan and friends. When it arrived at the thick double-pane glass of our big picture window it just kept on coming—right into the living room, flopping on the hardwood floor at our feet. And there in the smooth frame of our gorgeous mountain view was a neat hole the size of a Bing cherry.

We stood agape, our mouths hanging so far open we could have camped in them. Nick coagulated, dumbstruck, while sick dismay slid down his body from scalp to toes, eyes big as bear paws at his mistake.

We were shocked with surprise and relief. No one was hurt. But, oh, how he wanted a do-over.

We laughed. We cried. It became a part of us. We escaped harm, except for the fact that, yes, we had to take away the bow for awhile and ground him. But not for life. Live and learn.

Mistakes are the paths we take to live new truths.

There are two ends to a three-part arrow. The pointy part holds either a blunted practice tip or a razor-sharp blade that can kill things. The long middle part, the shaft, must be straight; because when it's bent in the slightest degree your arrow will never fly true again. You might as well put it out of its misery and send it to arrow heaven. The feathery part opposite the tip end is called the flight. It makes the shaft fly right—straight. Three feathers are attached equidistant on the flight. The feathers are died bright colors so that when your arrow lands, you can find it among fallen leaves or brick houses. If one feather falls off, another must be properly glued on before the arrow can fly straight again. It's obvious that all the parts of an arrow work in harmony.

When you pick up one end of an arrow, the other end follows.

Well, duh.

The School of Life is all about choices, and harmony is the school song. No matter how much you're a wishin' and a hopin' and a dreamin' for a different effect—you can pick your choice, but you can't pick your consequences. They are stuck together like tip, shaft and flight.

In the end, the kind of diploma we receive reflects choice and accountability. It's obvious by now that school is not out forever; obvious that we are never immune from peer pressure; obvious that the need to conform is so habitual that it barely pierces conscious consideration. It's obvious that we still feel shame at feeling loneliness, feeling that we don't fit in, feeling that we're different. It's obvious that wrinkles, puckers, and creases don't equal smarts.

Boomers talk about creating "Second Adulthood." Creation is how we find ourselves. This is nothing new. In high school, to be a Snorthauser sister, all you had to do was eat a piece of pizza with one whole anchovy on it. There were about 10 of us. I was Belva Snorthauser.

We create to fit in. With others, with ourselves. We recreate ourselves every day through our choices—the arrows we shoot at the targets we pick. Middle-age is not a good excuse for choosing stupid. Neither is boredom, sorrow, anger, revenge, disappointment, or wanting to be the class clown. Holey windows equal drafty house. Precise practice prevents poor performance. We own both holey windows and holey targets.

Contrary to the popular notion that we're *not* who we were then, we're just older, completely unrelated to our younger selves, we *are* who we were *and* older.

Like Captain Hook, I (and perhaps you) have a fear of that old ticking crocodile. Time never stops chasing me. My fears, my shallow desires, my weaknesses, my *tweenerness*, all discourage me from careful aim. I'm afraid that circumstances might overtake me before I make all the excellent choices my spiritual self craves. But honorable goals and a sense of self-worth persuade me to aim at the bulls-eye of what is chasing me down. Clear thinking, deep breathing, steady pacing and foresight always result in better accuracy. Gilbert Arland said: "When an archer misses the mark, he turns and looks for the fault within himself. Failure to hit the bulls-eye is never the fault of the target. To improve your aim, improve yourself."

Today is the day of your big do-over. Living the next half of our lives compared to the first half will be like *Chicken Fat* vs. P90X.

Here is what it means to be a BoomerTweener™, you who are too young to be old, too old to be young. Here is what my targets—from those of my childhood to those of my adulthood—have shown me clearly:

We can be our best selves through small choices that bring about great things.
We are capable of the journey.
We can find joy in the journey.
We can discern that pleasure lacks the excellence, the breadth or the depth that joy possesses.
We can make peace with conditions we can't change.
We can appreciate adversity as blessings to make us stronger.
We can understand the divine nature that God has placed within each of us.
We can right many wrongs within ourselves.

We can learn truths we didn't know we didn't know.

We can keep giving and growing, rather than taking and diminishing.

We can see the possibilities in ourselves and in other people.

We can teach our best, by example, to younger people around us.

We can retain commitment, nobility, moral values, and integrity.

We can play and have fun.

We can dream again.

(We can eat Pizza Puffs and red licorice for lunch without expecting to be Jack LaLanne at 93. And we can never be Meryl Streep—only she can be her.)

The synergy of faith, hope, love, resilience, and humor is crucial for everyone in the universe. Being young at heart but older in other places is a winning combination that, once unlocked, can produce the Peace and Joy Degree we've been working toward since high school. Cool.

And so if you never had a parent who was there to tell you what my parents counseled me, let me remind you...

Be good (Especially when others are being bad).
Be brave (Especially when others are being cowardly).
Be kind (Especially when others are being mean).
Be secure (Especially when others are being erratic).
Be wise (Especially when others are being foolish).
Be fun (Especially when others are being bored).

Remember who you are.

*   *   *

Inside every older person is a younger person wondering what happened.
-Steven Wright

In their 2008 April meeting, the American Physiological Society revealed that simply anticipating a humorous event (a funny movie, a good laugh) reduces three different stress hormones, increases human growth hormones (which boost immunity) and increases mood-elevating endorphins.

Laughter is to life what shock absorbers are to an automobile. It won't take the potholes out of life, but it sure makes the ride smoother.
-Barbara Johnson

I've Been 16 for 34 Years - BoomerTweener

Throwing Up
1955-2008

It's not every day you're compelled...
When you're nauseated, no matter what you do, *nothing*—not even picturing yourself on an Arabian gelding galloping bareback in the surf on a tropical sandy beach before dismounting to repose in a hammock under the shade where you sip a frosty lemonade brought to you by Jacques the pool boy—*nothing* will stop the gruesome smorgasbord of what you ate the previous 24 hours from parading through your mind.

The grizzly spectacle of foods chosen by your most beloved house guests (we love them but they don't love veggies) keep churning through your senses. A succession of greasy...a series of unfortunate events....

March, march, march, march...*for dinner...a* CHEESEBURGER smothered in special XXX sauce, FRIES, ketchup, and CHOCOLATE MALT!!

March, march, march, march...*for breakfast... English muffin with* BUTTER *and jam*, MILK, EGGS OVER-NOT-SO-EASY, and BACON!!

March, march, march, march...*for lunch after a sunny ferry ride to Bremerton...lemonade with* FISH & CHIPS *fried at the dockside greasy spoon!!*

March, march, march, march...*for dinner after a hot sunny ferry ride back home...a bucket o'* FRIED CHICKEN, POTATO SALAD IN MAYONNAISE, *fruit*, CHOCOLATE CAKE *with* PEANUT BUTTERY FROSTING, *and* ICE CREAM!!

Then *voilà!* Your stomach contents flash before your eyes—the Drum Majorettes of Greasy Regret. Could this misery come from the grandkids passing a flu bug around the past two weeks? Or say, four dump-truck loads of grease, salt, dairy, and sugar? No matter.

First you say *I am woman, is this heart attack?* Then you pray *please don't let me throw up.* But after six dark and stormy nighttime hours of sweating, tossing, turning, gurgling, and roiling with five false alarms, you pray *please don't let me throw up...but please, bless me with the runs...please!!*

Compelled by an odd force to evacuate essentials...nope, it's not every day you get to upchuck fascinating glimpses of your innermost self.

And writing *this* was a lot like *that*.

Trying to plan for the future without a sense of the past is like trying to plant cut flowers.
                    –Daniel Boorstin

It's amazing how grandparents seem so young once you become one.
                    -Author Unknown

Today is not yesterday: we ourselves change; how can our Works and Thoughts, if they are always to be the fittest, continue always the same? Change, indeed is painful; yet ever needful; and if Memory have its force and worth, so also has hope.
                    -Thomas Carlyle

With mirth and laughter let old wrinkles come.
                    -Shakespeare, *A Merchant of Venice*

How dull it is to pause, to make an end,
To rust unburnished, not to shine in use!
....
...Come, my friends.
'Tis not too late to seek a newer world.
Push off, and sitting well in order smite
The surrounding furrows….

....
We are not now that strength which in old days
Moved earth and heaven, that which we are, we are –
One equal temper of heroic hearts,
Made weak by time and fate, but strong in will
To strive, to seek, to find, and not to yield.

                        -Alfred Lord Tennyson
                        from the poem "Ulysses"

    There is a choice you have to make in everything you do.
And you must always keep in mind, the choice you make, makes you.
                        -Author Unknown

    It is not enough for a man to know how to ride; he must know how to fall.
                -Mexican Proverb

This is the true joy of life, the being used for a purpose recognized by yourself as a mighty one; the being thoroughly worn out before you are thrown on the scrap heap; the being a force of nature instead of a feverish selfish little clod of ailments and grievances complaining that the world will not devote itself to making you happy.

-George Bernard Shaw

Does your Book Club need a laugh or a cry?

Would you like to invite Julie Oliver to your book club discussion? She would love to visit! There are two ways to make it happen.

Video Conference -
Now that computers make it possible to connect through real-time video conferencing, this author can "drop in" to your book group. It's as easy as 1-2-3-4:
1. Order your books a couple months in advance.
2. Schedule your preferred conference date with the author.
3. Read! Finish *I've Been 16 for 34 Years* in time for your discussion with Ms. Oliver.
4. Coax our computer connections to join us on this literary adventure.

In Person -
Check our website *boomertweener.com* for details.
Check our websites for sample questions to guide your book club discussions.
Any book group that orders 10 or more books will receive 10% off the total order.

Funtime!

About the Author

"I was born under a Russet potato on the windswept plains of the Snake River Valley in southeastern Idaho. I saw stories in the billowed white clouds floating every day across brilliant blue skies. As a small child, I was inspired to write after listening to pioneer stories narrated by my grandparents; after feeling the humor and strength of my parents; after daydreaming on the back of my first bay pony; after reading my way into big towns, big jungles, big dramas; after playing dress-up as some new girl; after loving the wild acres we tamed to produce food for the world; after admiring the endurance of high desert farm families; after seeing God's hand in all of it."

Julie Oliver is the author of poetry, magazine articles, stage plays, and screenplays. She is an award-winning author, artist and photographer. This is her first big book. It was lots of work.

She is committed to drinking more water every day; catching a sixteen pound Chinook salmon; and sharing humor that uplifts, because Second Adulthood should be lived with joy.

She lives with eleven chickens, several cats, two dogs, one puppy, and one husband in the forests of Washington state, which also means, from time to time, they host wild things on their front porch—bears, coyotes, lynx, cougars, raccoons, foxes, deer, squirrels, chipmunks, birds, moles, voles, and gophers...and wild blackberries with thorns the size of darning needles.

Being a mountain man every day...er, a mountain *person* every day...makes it hard to feel urbane, as writers are thought to be.

There ain't much fun in medicine, but there is a heck of a lot of medicine in fun.
 -Josh Billings

**Order another book...it's the perfect gift!
Just tear out this sheet and mail to...**
Groveland Branch Press, PO Box 460, Fall City, WA 98024 USA.

It's easy to order books and merchandise from our websites...
boomertweener.com -or-
cafepress.com/boomertweener -or-
juliejoliver.com
-or-

Please send me the following books: I understand that I may return items within 10 days for a full refund if I'm not delighted with my purchase.

_____Quantity_____

Please print legibly:
Name_____
Address: _____
City:_____State:_____Zip:____
Telephone: _____
Email address: _____

Your information will not be sold or rented to third-party vendors.

Sales tax: Please add 9% sales tax.
S & H: Add $6.00 for first product and $3.00 for each additional product.
International: $15.00 for first product and $7.00 for each additional product.

Payment: Check -or- Money Order **Do not send cash.**

Credit Card: __Visa __MasterCard __AMEX __Discover

Name on card: _____
Credit card number: _____
Exp. Date: _____
Signature: _____

I've Been 16 for 34 Years - BoomerTweener

www.ingramcontent.com/pod-product-compliance
Lightning Source LLC
Chambersburg PA
CBHW032249150426

43195CB00008BA/383